Scottish Thoughts and Reflections Vol 1.

Since moving back to Scotland from South Africa in August 2018

David R B Nicoll

Biography:

David was inducted as an International Poet of Merit with the International Society of Poetry in America in 1997 and made it to the semi-finals of a poetry competition there between 2000 selected poets from all over the world. He has had poetry published in South African and International magazines and newspapers and was listed in the International Who's Who of Poetry in 2012. He has released a number of poetry books and CDs with poetry and music. All CDs to date recorded and produced in South Africa. Please check out his website with links to the books and CDs on www.davidnicoll.co.uk

This book released on 11th September 2019

Thanks to Jack Daly for the POKE, POetic joKE illustrations, if you would like any illustrations done, please contact him on jackdaly942gmail.com

Printed via Amazon.co.uk

First Printing, 2019

ISBN 0-9781687170170

www.davidnicoll.co.uk

david@davidnicoll.co.uk

We care about the planet and all lifeforms on it, we also object to many planes leaving long white streaks all over our skies and blocking out our sunshine amongst other things. Please join us if you do as well,

Facebook group:

SMAAPP Scottish Musicians and Artistes Against the Poisoning of our Planet

Index:

30!

Alright!

A Star!*

Above!

African!*

Again!*

And me!

Anymore!*

Are here!

Around!*

Back!*

Bars!*

Bee!*

Behind!*

Blind!

Block!

Blow!

Book launch!

Books!*

Buzzing!

Calamity!

Century!*

Clan!*

Coincidence!*

Commodity!

Consequences!

CONtrail!*

Crate!

Crow!*

Dead!*

* = with matching photograph

= with matching illustration

Degree!*

Despair!

Dis-Ease!*

Disease!

Dog walking!*

Dont know!

Double!*

Drum!

Eat!

Enough!*

Expire!

Face!*

Fine!

Fist!*

Flies!

Free!*

Frequencies!*

Game!*

Go!*

Geoengineering!*

Going down!

Hand!

Hay!

Head!

Here!

Him too!

History!

Hit!

Humanity!

I go!*

Immortalised!*

Insanity!

Irretrievably!*

It!

Key!

Lawyer!

Leg up!

Material!

Me!#

Memory!*

Mercury!

Move!

My leg!#

NoScabangosInStavanga!

Not on!*

Not see!*

Now!

Of it!

Omnicide!

Oran mor!*

Out!*

Pal!*

Pay!

Planting!*

Poetry!

Prevail!*

Rain!*

RAIN!*

Reality!

Regret!

Rent!

Rhino!*

Ride!*

Right!*

Salesman!*

Saturday!

Save!

Saw the Sun!

See!*

Seen!*

Sing!*

Sheets!

Sky!*

Sow!

Spray!*

Sprays!

Stars!*

Synchronicity!

Tattoos!*

Technology!

The Blues!

The day!

Thehardbard!*

The summer!

Them!

The Wild Arab!

Thistle!#

To me!

There!*

Three!

To see!

To see… Song lyrics!

To see! (3)

Today!

Two!*

Ultimately!*

Underground!*

Universe!

Vertically!*

Vinci!*

Waltzin the pencil!

What are these long white streaks in the sky?

Wit and me!*

Wolf!*

Work!#

Write up for book launch!*

Yes!#

What is it

About educated people,

That they just cannot,

Or will not see?

What is going on

Right over their

Heads

So frequently!

"What is that?"

You ask

Pointing at

A long white

Spreading trail

In the sky,

Plain for all to see!

"It is a CONtrail!"

They reply

Eloquently!

"It is

Empirical science!"

The one

Said to me!

Are they

Brainwashed?

The question

Came to me!

Why do they

Not see?

CONtrails

Nowadays

Are rare!

And short,

Absolutely

Nothing to

Compare!

And only for

A short while

Do they exist,

They do not

Criss cross the sky!

Birthed by planes

Spraying coal fly ash,

Mixed with other things,

While cruising

Oh, so high!

Then

Lo and behold

After spraying,

No more of the Sun,

Do you see!

As behind a white haze,

While below

Forests and

Houses blaze!

It is hidden

From sight,

Why,

Is no mystery!

Solar radiation

Management,

Stratospheric

Aerosol injection

And

Geoengineering,

Google these,

The truth to see!

Also, while

You are at it,

Look up the UNs

Agenda 21

And

30!

Alright!

"We got really

Bad news

Last Sunday!

A man who

Was there

Committed suicide

Just after our set!

Why he did this,

I don't know!

He didn't

Seem uptight!"

I then asked,

Jokingly,

Of course,

"Was

Your set

Alright?"

A Star!

A young

Norwegian girl,

Was banned

By her father,

From getting

A tattoo!

She was

Really pissed off!

But there was little

That she could do!

So,

When she was

In Bali,

From Norway

And her father

Very far!

She had

Under her foot,

Tattooed

A

Star!

He also banned

Her from getting

A belly button

Piercing,

This went

Right to her head!

So, she

Pierced

Her nipple

Instead!

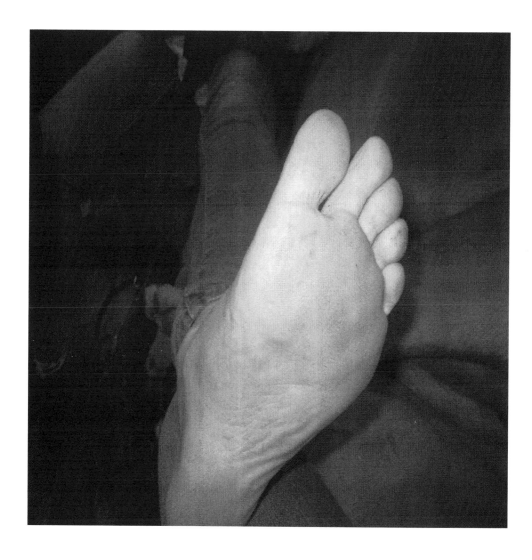

Above!

Had a real
Serendipitous
Night last night,
That much I know,
As I went to church
At Oran mor,
In Glasgow's west end
Now some happenings
Are getting me
Thinking more!
Got welcomed at the bar
By a handsome young man!
Looks like my own son,
He was bubbly,
Lightly ginger bearded
Lots of fun!
Looks like he could be
A star,
Then asked him,
"What do you do?"
He replied
"I am a singer,
Songwriter, and actor.
I also play guitar!"
"Got my break
By knowing a man called
Ronan Keating,
We co-wrote
Six of his songs
On his latest CD!
It was very successful!"
He said to me!
Just Google
www.danhealymusic.com
And then you will see!"
I was impressed,
I must say
"Pure Serendipity!"
"As I am poet,
Have been told
That I am a Bard!
Just returned
From South Africa
After thirty-six years,
Returning with many
Blessed moments

And creations
Was not hard!"
We both in our blood,
Need to create!
To make tangible
The invisible!
To give food to thought!
Mentioning everyday
Issues, dangers
Beauties and joys!

This is a new creation:

Spiritual realm above!

Starting as a small jolt
Of mental electricity!
It forms a thought
Which is
Creating and developing,
But is invisible to see!
As it is then
In the stage of
Mental imagery!
As the dream develops
In your mind
As if meant in fact,
To make the
Thought come true!
Then you need to act!
It doesn't matter,
Whatever it may be,
Nothing that was
Ever created by man
Had to go
Through someone's
Mental imagery!

A short poem:

Acheivement!

Imagination is the key
To light the fire!
As it comes before desire!
The seed bursts open
Many leaves to vent!

Then starts
The process of development,
Till your flower bursts open
Revealing your dream,
As if almost Heaven sent!
You have gone from a thought
To Achievement!

It is a pleasure to meet you Dan
And to record,
We must make a plan!
As I have done
In number three CD,
Like David Nicoll and friends,
Vols 1,2 and 3!
Please check out
www.davidnicoll.co.uk
As there are
The creations by me!

Another strange
"Co-incidence!"
Ended up reciting my poem,
"The time of your life!"
To you
And you were
Just involved with
A similar big
CD project with the same title!
Sending you this poem
With great feeling and love!
As Deepak Chopra says!
"Coincidences are
Only co-incidental to you!
They are clues
From the
Spiritual realm
Above!"

African!

Having spent most

Of my life in Africa!

Some habits

I cannot lose!

Now back in Scotland

When the Sun

Is shining,

Walking round

In bare feet,

Getting asked

"Where are your shoes?"

Well, I have always

Been able to

Makaplan!

And after

Thirty-six years there

Know that,

You can take

An African

Out of the bush,

But you can't

Take the bush,

Out of

An

African!

Again!

Now sitting

With a constant

High Pitch ringing

Inside my head,

It doesn't go away,

Even when

Lying in my bed!

It just never ceases!

The only variation,

Is that sometimes,

The volume increases!

Known as Tinnitus,

Both here

And overseas,

But to me,

I think that,

It is created

By EMFs!

Electro

Magnetic

Frequencies!

There is a reason

That this I say,

Because for two days,

In the

Scottish Highlands,

It went away!

What a pleasure that was,

I must say!

Now back in the city

And mores the pity,

Now must live

With this

Constant

Mental strain!

As soon

As I got back

To Glasgow,

The ringing

In my head,

Started

Again!

And me!

So tomorrow I will
Have my first taste
Of socializing
In Stavanger, Norway!
What lies ahead
In this place?
I cannot say!
Like everywhere I travel,
Fine people do I meet,
End up reciting poetry,
Or performing music
Which is sweet!
One day at a time
And all is fine,
After working hard
All week, tomorrow,
I shall drink some
Cider and wine!
Que sera sera,
What shall be shall be!
Looking forward
To developing,
The relationship
Further,
Between
Norway
And me!

Anymore!

I don't really have

An explanation for this,

It is so farfetched that it is

Almost beyond belief!

Last Wednesday night,

Bert and I were

At the Clusterfuck circus,

In Nice n Sleazy,

Sauchiehall street,

For poetry and comedy,

Invited by Oliver Pissed,

The organiser and

Ring master in chief!

We had a brilliant night,

Second to none,

Had a load of laughter

And lots of fun!

At the end,

All the

Performers got on stage,

For a crazy Celtic dance!

Uninhibited, free Spirits,

Loving life and

Making the most

Of the moment

And the

Circumstance!

Outside the pub

Was great as well,

While having

A smoke break!

I thought that I was

Back in Amsterdam,

Make no mistake!

The banter was brilliant,

As all that

Were there know!

A couple of joints

Were going around,

Having a

Sociable blow!

At the end of the evening

Bert heads off in a taxi

To his bed!

But I hung around,

Meeting, greeting

And with cider

Getting a wee bit

Oota ma head!

About an hour or so later,

It's time for me to roam,

And stop of at Church,

At Oran mor,

On the way home!

So, I say cheers to the poets

And comedians too!

Then head off to the busy

Taxi rank across the road,

Just before two!

Just jump in the first taxi,

They were in a long line,

Now half pissed,

A bit stoned,

But feeling fine!

"Are you a poet?"

The taxi driver

Asks me,

Before we had

Travelled far!

And I reply,

"Most certainly!"

"Do you know Bert Stables?"

"Indeed, I do!

Just left him here!"

Shit, if the taxi driver

Has heard of him,

He must be a local star!

So, in the morning

I get a call from Bert

Who was distraught,

"I lost my lifetime

Poetry books last night,

These are totally unique,

My lifestyle work,

Irreplaceable, unique,

They cannot be bought!"

He told me that

It hurt him so bad,

Tears were running

From his eyes,

Such a loss,

That he could not disguise!

His whole history of poetry,

Was now gone, he had left it

In his taxi on the way

Home to Denniston,

Tried to contact the taxi driver

But to no avail,

"There are

Lots of independent

Drivers there!"

Was the tale!

This led him to wail!

So, the taxi driver

That I got said to me,

"So, you know Bert Stables,

A wee bit earlier in my cab,

He left his poetry!"

My God, I am thinking

How can this be?

It is one of the biggest

Coincidences ever for me!

Now doubt it is beyond that,

In the realm of

Synchronicity or

Synchro destiny!

So tonight on

Your 74th birthday Bert

I have something here for you!

You and I both know the score!

Here are the

Collected Poetic works,

By a famous Glaswegian poet

Called Bert Stables,

Please photocopy the books

And don't carry,

The originals

Anymore!

Please note:

There are over 1 million people

Living in Glasgow

And 5000 taxis,

What are the odds of this happening?

LITTLE THINGS

LITTLE THINGS CAN MEAN A LOT
YOU TRY AND DO WHAT YOU WERE TAUGHT
TRY IS THE BIGGEST WORD I KNOW
YOU STOP AND THINK THEN GO BACK TO GO
THIS I LEARNED FROM MY DAD
HE HAD ALWAYS A SMILE AND NEVER SAD
NEVER COMPLAINED OR SAID POOR ME
WHEN YOU LOOKED THAT SMILE WAS ALL THAT YOU COULD S
EVERY TIME HE WENT OUT FOR A WALK
HE WOULD ALWAYS STAND AND HAVE A TALK
NICE DAY HE WOULD SAY
JUST TO PASS THE TIME OF DAY
WORRIES WERE GONE JUST FOR A WHILE
WHENEVER YOU LOOKED AND SAW THAT SMILE
MRS DO YOU WANT A HAND ACROSS THE ROAD
WORRIES WERE GONE JUST FOR A WHILE
WHENEVER YOU LOOKED AND SAW THAT SMILE
MRS DO YOU WANT A HAND ACROSS THE ROAD
TAKING HER BAGS AND LIGHTNING HER LOAD
LIKE FILLING THE BOWL FOR YOUR DAUGHTER
JUST TO GIVE THE STRAY DOG A DRINK OF WATER
GIVE THE OLD WOMAN'S DOOR A KNOCK AND SAY HELLO
DONT JUST RUSH BY TO AND FRO
WOULD YOU LIKE ANY MESSAGES HEN
IL WRITE THEM DOWN IF YOU GIE ME A PEN
BACK TO HER DOOR YOU WOULD COME
THEY HAD NAE BREED LEFT HEN BUT IL GIE YOU SOME
UP TO THE HOOSE YOU WENT FOR YOUR PIE BEANS AND CHIPS
YOU ATE THE LOT AND LICKED YOUR LIPS
SO NEVER BE FRIGHTENED OF GROWING OLD
FOR ALL THESE STORIES CAN ALWAYS BE TOLD

B Stubbs ©
14/6/10

Are here!

Rob,

That spray

You showed

Yesterday,

Was very low

In the sky!

As if almost

Directly

Over the top

Of the houses,

The plane did fly!

All the people

Getting ready,

To lie in bed!

Without realising

That after

Breathing it in,

The Nanoparticles

In the spray

Will become

Lodged,

Inside your body,

And the aluminium

Coalesced

In your head!

I do not say this

To create fear!

But when I saw it,

My thoughts were,

That in

Biblical terms

The end times

Are here!

Around!

Tired of having

My drink taken away,

When I am in the toilet

And not to be found!

So, I now

Leave this message

On top of my drink,

So that,

When I return,

It is still

Around!

Back!

Rewind music festival

At Scone Palace,

Perthshire,

Is really a blast,

Great performers

And people making

Memories last!

Listening to the stars

From the eighties,

Bringing into the present,

Sounds and vibrations

From the past!

Paul Young, Foreigner

And Lulu too!

Bringing their magic

To share,

With me and you!

Set in the palace ground,

With peace,

Beauty and nature

All around!

This is great crack!

Looking forward to

Listening to

Midge Ure,

The Undertones

And Brian Ferry,

Then God willing,

Next year,

I will

Be

Back!

Bars!

Having just come back

From South Africa,

Such a sight as this,

Over there,

I had never

Come across!

These keys

Were left

Lying, right

Outside the door!

Been there for weeks,

Nobody moved them

Or tried them,

Not many thieves

Or housebreakers around

Obviously,

You know the score!

Another world over here

Under northern stars,

When in the

Southern Hemisphere

You live in peace,

Behind your own

Burglar

Bars!

Bee!

Natures

Pollinators,

Exchanging and

Capturing

Pollen as

They go!

Since time

Immemorial,

They have been

Going with the flow!

Flying from

Flower to flower,

Doing what they do!

Cross pollinating

Many flowers,

Vegetables,

Bushes

And trees

As only

They know!

Now there

Is a threat,

Which is really

Not funny!

Against these

Providers

Of Honey!

mm Microwaves

Kill them,

Which is really

Not good!

Because

If they

Disappear,

Then not

Long after

We humans,

Will be short

Of food!

Many millions

Are dying!

Leaving

Apiarists sighing!

And

Honey makers

Crying!

The reason

For this you see,

Is the introduction

Of 5G!

We can do

Without

Faster internet

Download speed,

That much

I see!

But we

Cannot

Do

Without,

The

Bee!

Behind!

A mere six months ago

I was without a home

In Mossel bay,

The garden route

In South Africa

Sleeping in my

Old red 1994 Mercedes,

Free to roam!

But having run out of money,

Things were not funny!

Had been living in

Lake Brenton, Knysna,

Without a job for a year

After retrenchment

But feeling fine,

Practicing retirement

With my honey,

We shared great times

In beautiful mountains,

Beaches, live music scenes

And sharing more

Than one bottle of wine!

Great times without a doubt,

That is until,

The money runs out!

"What now?

Where do we go?"

So back to Mossel bay,

Which is where

We used to stay!

Not used to this situation,

That much I could see,

Lying under a duvet cover,

On the laid-back front seat

Parked in a quiet street,

Under the shade of a tree!

Only going there after dark,

Parking opposite

To a backpackers

Next to a park!

"What is next?

What can I do?"

Mentally panicking

On a park bench

With no income,

No job and no home,

But at least I was not alone!

Together Shakeenah

And I held our power!

We would go down

To the sea water

Swimming pool

At the Point in the morning,

To share a

Rejuvenating cold shower!

Food becoming scarce,

Eating lowly just to survive!

Sold or threw away

All my possessions,

Just to stay alive!

My family of djembe drums

With carved faces,

Shaka and The Mistress

To sell them, it took long!

They ended up in a

Knysna second hand store

Along with my Tibetan singing bowls,

The whole lot went for a song!

Sitting by the side of the Knysna lagoon,

Makes an interesting tale,

Sitting for hours

And days with on the windscreen,

A sign saying

"For sale!"

Low moments in my life,

Long time on my own

Without a legal wife!

Had been holding on

With the possibility

Of getting my job back,

At the Mossel bay

Gas to Oil refinery!

"I have to leave Africa!"

The thought almost

Brought me to tears!

As I had been

Living and loving,

The place and people

For over thirty-six years!

But one thing that sticks

Badly in my mind!

Is that I had to leave

My beautiful young lady

Behind!

Blind!

"I have a movie

To show you tonight!

It is a true story!"

This brightened

Up his wife's eyes!

Gave her delight!

But when she saw

That it was

A blue movie,

It turned

Things out

Not right!

"You want me

To do what?"

"Are you

Out of

Your mind?"

She then

Slapped him

In the ear

And almost

Made

Him

Blind!

Block!

I am reading

It in the news

And listening

To people talk,

A massive heatwave

Is supposed to hit

The UK soon,

Just wondering,

Are the pilots

Going on holiday

During that period,

And not spraying

Anymore

Sun

Block?

Blow!

Did the red-light district

In Amsterdam last night!

It was fokkin brilliant,

In many small

Brightly lit windows

Were many

A beautiful alluring,

Feminine sight!

They are there waving at you,

Trying to allure you,

As many people,

In the narrow streets

Mingle through!

Some beauties there,

That much I can say!

With all of them doing it

To bring home some pay!

Of course, having visited

A Coffee shop beforehand

And having a blow,

I was now feeling

Better than OK!

Passed the one

Beautiful blonde,

Who smiled and

Waved so cute!

Sitting on a stool,

Behind glass in a doorway,

Wearing a sexy black nightie

And a G string,

Over her birthday suit!

I wonder

How much she charges?

This beautiful dear,

As her body

For sure,

I would love to hold near!

So, for her at the doorway

My face did suddenly reappear!

"It is only fifty Euros,

For a roll my dear!"

Now me,

I have already had my brood!

And thought, Poor lady,

She is no doubt doing it

To get her kids some food!

So, from a philanthropic

Point of view!

The curtain was

Drawn at her door

And I walked through!

"You must pay me first!"

Was her immediate outburst

As up to her bedroom we go!

She is unwrapping a condom,

Slipping it on and

Then giving me a blow!

So, me on my back

My mind going off track,

Stoned brain but very happy,

"Are you ready for sex now?"

She asks,

Then proceeds to mount me!

I am thinking,

"Wow, she really has some body!"

Being a natural thing,

As writing poetry in rhyme!

I try to squeeze her tits

At the same time!

"No baby,

You pay extra for that!

Sorry my honey,

But if you want to do that

Then you must

Pay me more money!"

This is extortion!

The thought through my

Mind it did pass!

"Do I have to pay extra as well

To squeeze your ass?"

"Would you like to lick my pussy?"

Well, to be honest, I did!

As my hands, round her

Vibrating ass I slid!

But being Scottish and talking

In a cultured accent of note!

I asked her,

"Could you give me a quote"

It was very handy I must say,

My body now sweating,

With temperature rising

Aa an orgasm I was getting!

A community service,

Creating temporary bliss!

Then telling her

"I am a poet,

I am going to write

About this!"

So, after a while

Feeling empty ballbags

And all over sweet!

I am once again walking

In an Amsterdam street!

"What a place this is

I will have you know!

In the last couple of hours

I have legally got laid

And scored

Some really

Nice Blow!"

Book launch at the Glasgow Literary lounge,

Calton bar on Tuesday 28th May 2019

Having just returned from over thirty-six years in South Africa, a lot of my work there has been to do the wildlife in Africa and the challenges that it faces. Numerous poems of mine have been dedicated to this subject; I will be reciting some of them.

Value adding to poetry is also a pet subject and I like to add matching photographs, illustrations and music to go with them ultimately, one can do a lyric video after the music has been added. For example, please look up I wish just for today on YouTube.

Poetry can also be made into songs. I did lots of lyrics for songs, please have a listen to Mervyn Fuller and David Nicoll, Poetic and musical collaboration CDs and David Nicoll and friends Vols. 1, 2 and 3. All links on www.davidnicoll.co.uk

POKEs POetic joKEs are a favorite of mine, I love to make people laugh and POKEs is a great way of doing that. I will be covering small sections of each of the above subjects as well as releasing my latest book, Thoughts and Reflections Vol 3 and will also have copies of my previous books and CDs on hand.

Books!

There is a bar lady

Called Grace,

Who I have met!

Who's features

Are Viking set!

She has a really

Lovely glow!

And keeps me happy,

With a humbling glow!

There is only

One thing,

That I would

Like to know?

If she wants to see

Her image online,

Then please let me

Take the photo!

She is pretty,

With lovely looks,

And I do photos

Of people,

For the

Website,

Reviewing,

My

Books!

Buzzzing!

Was just saying

To a friend in Glasgow,

While talking about,

The switching on

Next month of 5G!

That it should be

A very interesting time

As far as I can see!

What with

All the spraying

Going on

From planes above,

With Nano particles

Of Aluminium,

Barium and Strontium,

They are certainly not

Put there in love!

They will now

Be in our bloodstream

Also, our brain!

This is sure to create

Some strain!

We may well

Never recover,

Or be healthy

Again!

He plays

for a band,

Likes to hit

The djembe drum

And sing!

Said to him that

This time

Next month,

We could be

Buzzing!

Calamity!

This is a message!

For ALL of humanity!

For every lifeform,

Animal, fish,

Bird, insect

And tree!

Regardless of your

Minor differences,

Whatever

They may be!

Things are happening,

Threatening

All our futures,

It can only

Be described,

As pure,

Insanity!

Put in place,

By the

Powers

That be!

Spraying poisons

In all our skies,

Incessantly!

Yet these

Long white

Criss crossing

Trails in the sky,

The majority

Of the people,

Just do not see!

Please,

Look up!

Wake up!

Question

What you see!

Link up,

Before

The

Calamity!

Century!

Twa Glesgae legends

As far as I can see!

Outside the Scotia bar,

In Glasgow,

Which was

Already open

In the year of

Seventeen

Ninety-three!

Bert Stables, poet

And percussionist

Extraordinary!

And Ian Hamilton;

Famous

Folk singer,

Wearing a kilt

From the

Thirteenth

Century!

Clan!

End up with a loose

Lower tooth,

"As well to take it out!"

The dentist said to me!

"Aye well, ok then,

Makes no difference to me!"

"We will add more teeth

Onto your lower denture!"

Says he to me!

"Come back in a couple of weeks

And we will have another session,

Then I will take an impression!"

So back I go,

Mouth open,

Getting impression set,

When he told me something,

That made me quite upset!

"We will need

To have the denture

For four days!"

Is what he did say!

My reply being

"What?

But this is Friday!

No way!"

So, he gave

Two numbers to me,

One of which

Turned out

To be,

Johnny boy at

Glamorous Geggie!

Well, now this man,

Is a character to see!

"I have been operating

From this shop,

Since nineteen seventy-three!

When I arrived here,

I had long curly brown hair!"

Although the years

Have treated him well,

And with his work,

He is indeed a

Master craftsman

And takes great care!

Working away most of the time,

Creating dentures takes a while!

But after the wait,

Everyone leaves

With a new smile!

So if your dentures

Are giving you problems

And you live near Glasgow way!

Get Glamorous Geggies

To fix you up,

In only one hour,

Is what I say!

Which is an

Awful lot better

Than having

A half empty mouth

For more than one day!

We have

Something in common

As it turns out,

In the form

Of our surname

As they are

Almost the same!

He is Nicol,

I am Nicoll!

But there is an

L

Of a difference!

I really, really,

Like this man,

We obviously

Come

From a

Similar,

But ever so

Slightly,

Different

Clan!

Coincidence!

Just had a Coincidence

Of gigantic proportion

Happened to me!

It started with Intuition,

Google, Gordon Dickson,

Why I don't know,

But I did and found

Him on LinkedIn

Fortunately!

We grew up

In our teenage years

In Mountcastle,

Edinburgh,

Hadn't seen him

In many a year!

Made contact,

Arranged to meet

Which would bring us

And my other friend Morey,

Lots of good cheer!

So, we meet up

And go to the Scottie,

At the end of the Broadway

To sink more than

Just one beer!

So great

To once again meet,

All of us enjoying,

The jokes,

The memories,

The blether!

The chip shop

Is still there!

That surprised me so,

As I used to get

Deep fried

Pizza suppers there

With three pickled onions,

Before leaving there over,

Forty-four years ago!

We were all

Looking a bit older,

That's for sure

And as far as I know,

No one has for

Ageing,

Come up with a cure!

Great to meet again,

Many memories of when

We would get up

To mischief,

Or when we used

To go up town to jive!

With a great thankfulness,

For us all still

Being alive!

Stayed the night

With Gordon,

Who lives near

The Friggie burn,

So, in the early afternoon,

To the Friggate park,

I made a turn!

Memories flooding back,

How we used to jump

From side to side,

Or swing from the trees

Over the burn,

With young hearts

Beating inside!

Sometimes we would

Go home filthy

And soaked,

Mud up legs,

Grotty shoes

And our

Duddingston primary

School clothes

Needing washed,

Our mothers

Would chide!

Heard that there were

Now Otters in the park!

Well, there never

Used to be,

So, I asked a passer-by

Walking her dog,

"Can you tell me

About the Otters?

Please lady!"

She said that

"There were

In number three,

That they eat the ducks,

Which is not funny!"

Also,

"They are difficult to see!"

Explained to her that it was

Fifty years since I had

Been in this park!

And

"Where did you

Used to stay?"

She asked me,

"I used to live in

Mountcasle Cresent!"

"What number?"

"In number

Thirty-three!"

"This cannot be!"

She said to me!

"That is my house!

Have lived there

For twenty-one years!"

She said to me!

"Would you like to

Come around

For a cup of tea?"

Walking away from her

With totally disbelief,

Thinking

"This cannot possibly be!"

After having read

Deepak Chopras book

Called Synchro destiny!

As a Coincidence,

Is only a Coincidence

To you,

You see!

He says that it is

Clues from

The Spiritual realm,

Like Synchronicity!

So, I go back to Gordon's

House and tell him,

"Before you drop me off,

I have been invited

By a lady

That I met in the park,

To pop in and have

A cup of tea!"

"That's fine!" he said,

"Alright by me!"

It was surreal,

Visiting once more,

My old family home,

Filled with many

A memory!

"I drew the extensions

For this home

And we built it ourselves,

My father and me!"

Going through

The dining room

Into the very fashionable

Scullery!

Then upstairs

To my old bedroom

Oh Lord,

How can this be?

Even Gordon told Charlotte

"I wish I had a pound for every

Time, I have been in this house!"

So, it wasn't just strange for me!

Why I don't know!

Of that,

I cannot make sense!

This to me,

Can only be

A

Gigantic

Coincidence!

Please clarify my thought,

So that of this,

I can

Make sense!

01.05.2019

Commodity!

Nowadays water

Companies

Make their money

For free!

They don't produce

Water,

They merely

Tap it,

Treat it

And

Bottle it!

All that they

Produce

Going ahead

At full throttle,

Are millions

Upon millions

Of plastic

Bottle!

The best bank

That has

Ever been found!

With all the water

Being taken

For free,

From the ground!

Nestle,

Even want

To patent it,

This is crazy,

As far as

I can see!

With clean

Drinkable water,

Probably being

The most valuable

Natural,

Essential,

Life giving,

Commodity!

Consequences!

Life is full

Of options,

If you can see

Where

The sense is?

And as

Bert Stables

Says,

"Choices

Are always

Followed

By consequences!

And if you

Make the

Right choices,

You will

Always get

The right

Consequences!

CONtrail!

What on earth

Do we have to do?

To get the world to see?

That these long white

Streaks, spreading

Across the sky,

Are not put there

Innocently!

They are not put there

For no reason,

They are not put there

For fun!

One of the reasons is

To block out the Sun!

This they do

Most definitely!

As the Sun

Gets hidden behind

A hazy screen,

As all can see!

They are sprayed

Across almost

Every nation!

Coal fly ash and

Other things

Is what they are,

Taken for free,

From many

Power stations!

They contain,

Nano particles

Which when breathed in

Can lodge in your brain!

The very fact,

That this is being done,

Is absolutely,

Insane!

Barium, Strontium

And Aluminium too!

Affects all living

Lifeforms on this planet,

As we daily pass through!

What can you do?

Well please think about it,

That would be a start!

Wonder how your children

And grandchildren's

Future will be,

When you are apart!

This is done

With malice,

Not with love!

For if it is

Not allowed

To go up a

Power stations

Chimney stacks,

Then why should

It be sprayed above?

Dementia and

Alzheimer's deaths

Now going off the scale,

Bees, insect's plants, trees,

Also dying off!

This spraying is creating

Global DIS -EASE!

Weather manipulation,

Is also part of the game,

Without a doubt,

Creating, cyclones,

Snowstorms, hurricanes,

Floods and drought!

It is almost enough

To make you wail!

When you ask someone

"What is that?"

And they reply

"A CONtrail!"

Crate!

Hugh is going

To retire soon!

For his working life

It is getting late!

He was just

Saying how,

When he

Was younger,

He used to have

A six pack!

But now

He has got,

A

Crate!

Crow!

A little fact

That not

Many know!

When a

Hebridean

White tailed

Sea eagle

Shows up,

It gets

Attacked,

In the air,

By a

Crow!

Photo by Chris Murray!

Dead!

"We were in a cage with

Fully grown Tigers!"

Was the story told to me!

And they had

Photos to prove it,

To me on hearing it,

To do that is insanity!

For Tigers are wild animals,

You never know,

What might set

Them off in a rage!

I mean you don't get

Members of the public,

Going into a

Lions cage!

Well, they used to

Put people into Lions cages

Which really didn't do them

Any good,

As they were being

Put there,

To become

The Lions food!

But here are,

The photos

To prove that they did

What they said!

They went into a

Fully grown Tigers

Cage in Thailand

And came

Out alive,

Not

Dead!

Degree!

At the

Findhorn

Foundation

In Scotland!

A recycling

Masterpiece

I did see!

Where all organic

Waste is recycled,

Then natural

Organic food,

Is grown,

For free!

The waste,

Is put into

Expanded

Polystyrene

Cookers,

Which

Make

Compost,

Very

Quickly!

At a hot

35

Degree!

Despair!

It is called Tinnitus,

A ringing in the ears!

Mainly gets you,

In your later years!

But it can drive you crazy!

Stop you from feeling fine,

As the ringing is there,

All of the time!

All during the day,

Or when

Lying in your bed,

You have this constant,

High pitched ringing,

Inside your head!

Sometimes life

Is not fair,

You stick your fingers

In your ears,

And the ringing

Is still there!

Oh Lord!

This is creating

Despair!

Dis-Ease!

Just saw a

New thing today!

Two planes flying

An identical course,

One slightly

In front and higher

Than the other,

With both,

Releasing long white

Dissipating spray!

From the ground it would

Appear that

There is only one trail!

But they will be intermingling

Into one as on the winds

These Nano particulates sail!

Why does nobody

See these things?

Or even wonder why?

Planes leaving

Long white spreading streaks,

All over our sky!

This observation made

In the Isle of Mull,

In the Inner Hebrides!

At peace with nature,

Mind and body at ease!

While these b#stards

In the sky spray ultimate

Death and

Dis-Ease!

Disease!

Just got thinking

About all the crap

That they

Spray in our sky!

At altitudes

That are very high!

And wondering

If on a

Lovely sunny day,

That the pilots

Of commercial aircraft

Are likely to say!

"Open the window a bit,

Let's feel the breeze!"

As they

Cruise along,

With the

Greatest of ease!

For if they do,

It would be

A mistake!

As into their lungs,

All these chemicals

They would take!

It is all very well

To be happy,

To feel

The fresh air and

Cooling breeze,

But not worth it,

If the Nanoparticles

Of Aluminium

End up coagulating

In their brain

And leaving them,

With dementia

Or

Alzheimer's

Disease!

Dog walking!

In Scotland

Often,

Getting

Around in

All weather

Can be a slog!

This gives

A new

Meaning

To,

"Honey,

I am

Just

Going

To

Walk

The

Dog!"

Don't know!

Learning a new

Computer programme,

When you start,

It is slow!

Then get advice,

From a helpful

Lady co-worker,

"Just give me a shout,

If there

Is anything

That you don't know!

Just let me know!"

"Well, how do I know?

What I don't know?

If you don't know,

What you

Don't know?"

Double!

This

Poor man

Must have

Vision

Trouble,

Here,

It looks

Like

He is

Seeing

Double!

Mark Whitby comment on Facebook:

I am having a big party, what will you bring?

Starting with the first letter of your name?

Drum!

Let me see,

What would it be?

Something beginning

With the letter D,

I could bring something

Which brings us laughter,

Happiness and hope

And bring along

A wee bankie

Of Dope,

Then again

You know us musos,

We like to

Sing and hum,

How could i forget,

I would also bring

My

Djembe

Drum!

Eat!

Met this young lady

On a

Dating site!

She looked cool,

Hope that everything

Works out right!

Sent her a message,

"Hi, you I would

Like to meet!

And the tattoo

On your chest

Looks really neat!"

This was over

Three months ago,

Time passes

Quite quickly,

Not at all slow!

Well for one reason

Or another,

We have still to meet!

But all being well,

We now have a date,

For next Friday night

To go out,

In Glasgow

And eat!

Tweet by Nicola Sturgeon 0n 08.07.2019

"Scottish summer sunset,

Love the light at this time of year!"

Enough!

"Love the light

At this time of year!"

The trails in

Front of the Sun

Will bring everyone's

Demise closer

And will not

Bring them

Any good cheer!

Are they

Natural cloud forms?

Or were they

Birthed by a plane?

Increasing dementia

And Alzheimer's

As the Aluminium

Nano particles

Inside them,

Once inhaled,

Coagulate and lodge

In your brain!

But being at the top,

Must be tough,

So, let's just agree!

"Aye, it's a fine Sunset

Right enough!"

Expire!

Whatever

You can do,

To light

Another's

Fire!

To

Raise

Their

Desire!

You

Should

Aspire!

To

Inspire!

Before

You

Expire!

Face!

The Scotia Bar!

A famous part

In Glasgow's history!

First opened in the year,

Of seventeen eighty-two!

With at that time,

All the

Modern convenience,

That you needed

To see you through!

A men's only bar,

No women allowed,

Within its

Hallowed door!

Brass hooks were hung

To hang you jacket or coat,

Right at the bar as on

Another wee dram

Or beer,

Your mind would float!

Brass Match lighters,

Screwed on

Just beneath the bar top,

Used by many in their time

Whose smoking habit,

They did not

Want to stop!

Solid wood columns,

Carved woodwork of note,

And a musical atmosphere,

That many can quote!

Great people and bar!

The home of

Many a home grown,

Music star!

Lots of laughter,

Many play instruments

And sing,

By the look of

The cash,

Hanging

From pegs,

Above the bar,

They are now

Into Money,

Laundering!

But the

Piece de resistance,

About this

Places history,

That not many know!

Is that in the old days

Recycled beer,

Through the bar

Would flow!

At the bottom

Of the bar front,

Still there to this day,

For all to see,

Is a trough,

Where the men,

Used to pee!

As some would say!

Pure Luxury!

If you are looking

For live music,

This is the place!

The Scotia!

You are sure

To leave,

With a smile,

On your

Face!

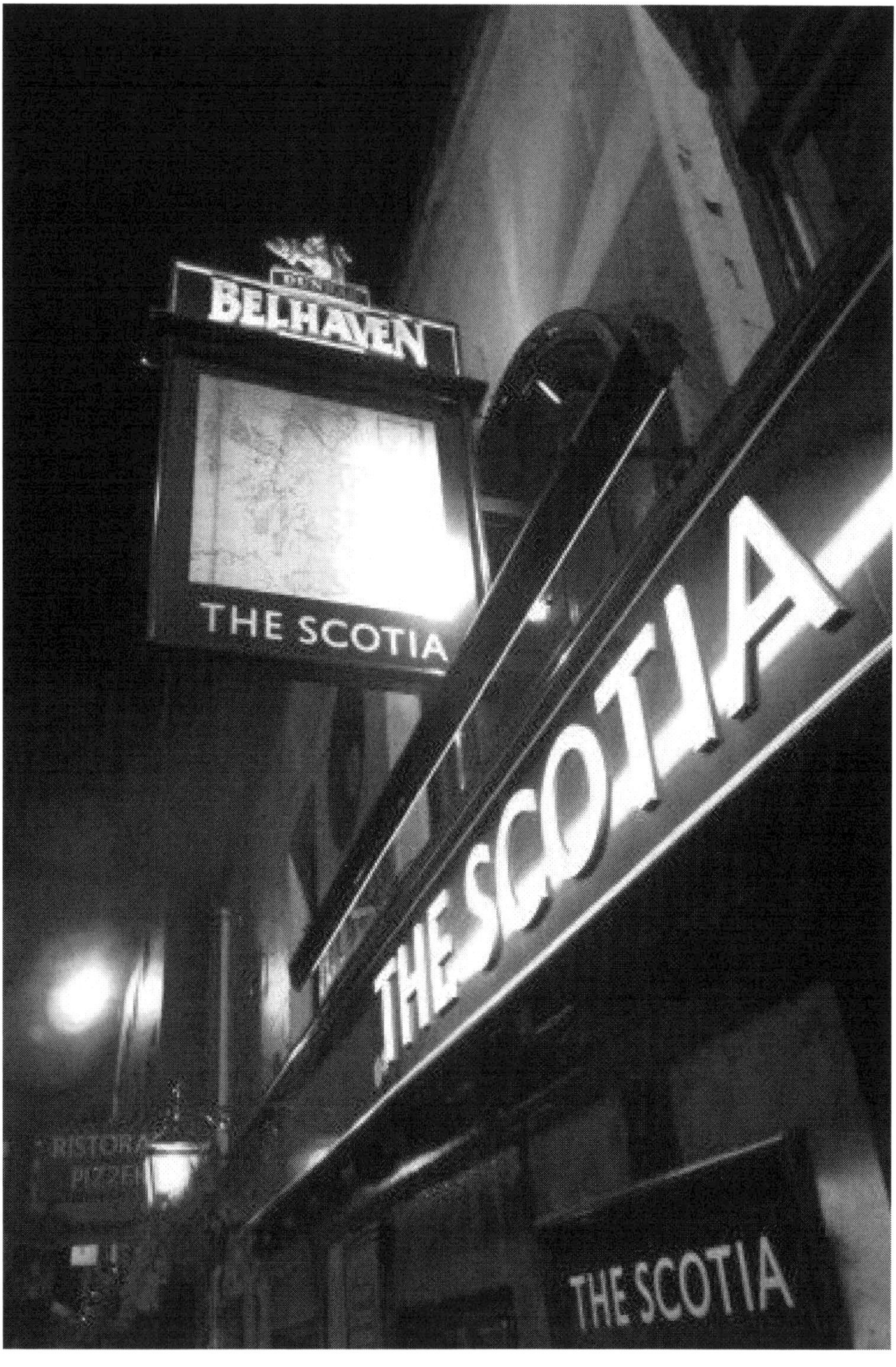
BELHAVEN
THE SCOTIA
THE SCOTIA
THE SCOTIA

Fine!

Please send me
All the details,
Of what that
I must do,
To do a transfer
To you!
You know that
I like to write,
In rhythm,
Meter and rhyme!
So, there is
A poetic question,
Which when
Answered
And the
Kilt made,
From the
Massai tartan,
I will be looking
And feeling
Fine!

Fist!

Met a man in

Stavanger, Norway

And this is what

He had to say!

"I have fifty-five

Tattoos on my body,

All on the one side!

Like the light and dark!

One side for love,

The other,

For the

Fighting spark!

Great to meet him,

The moment

I would not

Have missed!

One plain

And the other,

A heavily

Tattooed

Fist!

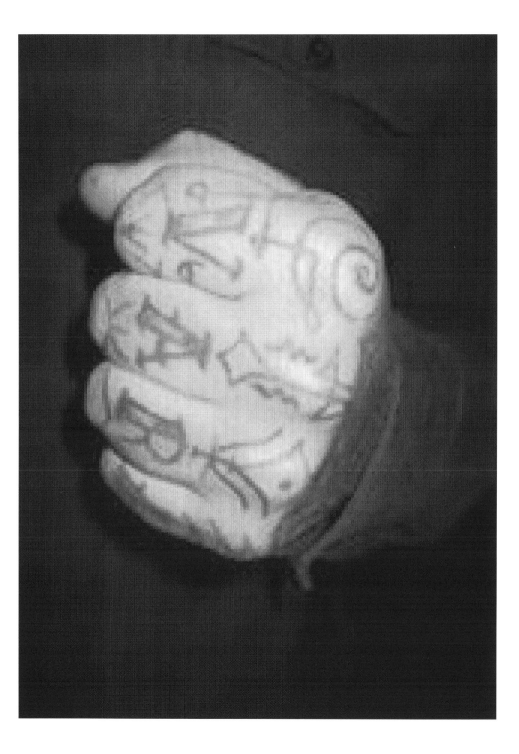

Flies!

Long white

Spreading streaks,

Being sprayed

In our skies,

Creating death from

Dementia and Alzheimer's,

As the weather channels

Tell us lies!

People dropping off

The mortal coil,

Like

Flies!

Free!

A revolution is brewing

Make no mistake!

As millions of Scots

Want freedom

From The union

And Westminster rule!

That they are

Prepared to take!

Tired of being treated

Like pawns in the game!

Where your opinions

Are disregarded,

It's always the same!

The Scottish MPs

In Parliament,

Are rarely

Listened too!

There is little

That they can do!

As if their input

Doesn't matter,

Just the Whisky,

Oil and tourism

Revenues make the

National fiscus fatter!

Forcing Brexit

Down the throats

Of a proud country,

That does not want it,

Will have its

Repercussions,

As they will see!

As once again,

As in

Ancestry!

Scotland,

Will

Be

Free!

Frequencies!

What are

These strange

Cloud shapes

In the

Scottish skies?

Also spreading

Over the seas!

Got one reply

That it was

Bagpipe

Reverberations,

But it could

Also,

Be

EMFs,

Electro

Magnetic

Frequencies!

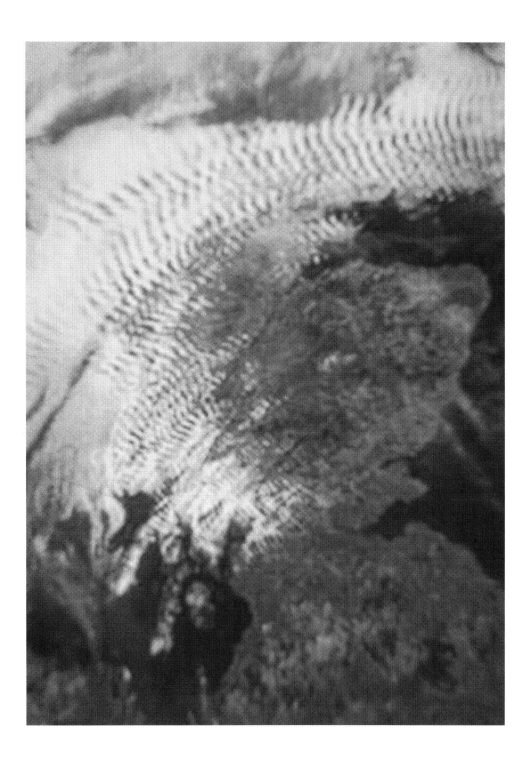

Game!

Just a very small

Percentage of people

In this beautiful

Scottish land,

Have gathered together

As

Anti-Geoengineering Scotland!

To awaken all the others

To threats

That they neither see,

Nor understand!

But they are aware

Of the threat

From the sky,

Showing itself

As many

Long white spreading streaks

Which cover our Sun

And sky!

Spread by anonymous planes,

But with government consent

That much we know!

As if it wasn't agreed to,

Then these planes,

From the skies

Our Air Force would blow!

Why do so few know?

Are you getting sick?

Are you feeling weak?

The doctor's attention

For one unknown reason

Or another

Do you need to seek?

Do you have a buzzing

In your head?

Even while

Lying in bed?

Or is there someone

That you know,

That to hospital must go?

Suffering from Dementia

Or Alzheimer's?

Creating in their families

Lots of grief and pain!

Both ultimately caused,

By a coagulation

Of Aluminium

Nano particles,

In your brain!

How did this happen?

You might well sigh,

Well the reason

Is because these particles

Came from the sky!

Many, many families now

Affected, never again

To be the same,

As we are all just

Pawns in the

Illuminati`s

Game!

Go!

Three poets

And percussionists

In a row,

Your time

On this planet

Is limited,

So,

Let the music

And poetry

Flow!

Before its

Your turn,

To

Go!

Jim Ferguson, Bert Stables and a Sumo Wrestler in training!

Geoengineering!

The majority of people

On this beautiful planet,

All with their own lifestyles,

Culture, religion,

History and tales!

When they see these,

Long white streaks,

In the sky,

They think

Nothing of them

And call them

CONtrails!

Busy with their lives,

Busy in their actions!

Minds being taken over,

By one or another

Modern day,

Distractions!

Never thinking

Of what is going on

Above their head!

Both during the daytime

And when

Lying in bed!

Up to no good,

These planes spread

Nano particles,

Of Aluminium,

Barium and

Strontium,

Which are not good,

For either you,

Or your brood!

They call it

Geoengineering!

Does that

Make a bell ring?

They are not

Doing this for fun!

One of their aims

Is to block out

The Sun!

This it does

Most successfully!

As after a

Couple of hours,

After spraying,

The Sun,

You cannot see!

Which leaves mankind

Lacking in

Intake of,

Vitamin D!

Consisting of

Coal fly ash

And other

Nasty things,

There will be

Hell, to pay,

When the dawning

Of this knowledge

In Humanity

Rings!

Although

When it will happen?

We have not got a date,

But if it is not soon,

That everyone

Wakes up,

Then I have a feeling

That it might be

Too late!

Some things

That these sprays

Can do to you!

Look out for

These symptoms,

In your family,

Friends,

Or even in you!

For they are true!

It will make people sick,

That is for sure!

These are some of

The things

That affect people,

From Nano particle

Exposure!

This will disturb them,

They will not be at ease!

With Neurological,

Parkinson's,

Or Alzheimer's

Disease!

Dementia is another

That is what they say,

Why is it now,

The number one killer

Of women in the UK?

Bronchitis, Asthma,

Emphysema

And cancer too!

When you

Breathe it in,

There is little

That you can do!

Heart disease,

Dermatitis,

Kidney and liver

Disease!

Will leave you

Bed ridden

And not feeling

At ease!

So, wake up,

Shake up!

And lift your head high!

Look at what is happening

Above your heads,

In your sky!

We are all

In this together,

There is no

Plan (et) B!

We must save

The future for our children

And our Mother Earth!

As there is nothing

That could be

Of more worth!

So next time

For your education,

While in your

Computer screen

Or cell phone

You are peering!

Please,

Google

Geoengineering!

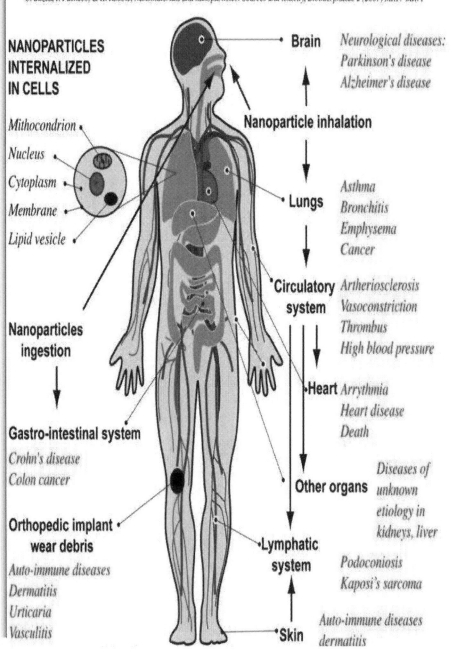

Going down!

Sitting on my own
In the car
At the end of a
Mossel bay street!
Presently my
Temporary home,
My lady missing,
Life has been more sweet!
Reminiscing of things
That have been and gone!
Days of nature,
Laughter and love,
Musical synchronicity,
Days of fun!
Now my cash has run out
We are on the run!
Creating gossip
In this small town!
Running overdue
Tabs in restaurants,
Spotted sleeping
In the morning
At garage,
Car park and park,
Leaving a frown!
If we are not going up,
Then we are surely
Going down!

Hand!

Circumstances

And situations,

Can sometimes

Leave you

With frustrations,

Possibly,

Palpitations!

Sometimes,

You have

No other option

Than to move

To one,

Or another nation!

This happens to lots,

You are not alone!

Although fear,

Can sometimes

Chill you,

To the bone!

To be uprooted,

Either through

Circumstance,

Situation,

Or choice!

Can lead you

To raise

Your voice!

It can be traumatic,

Leaving loved ones

Behind,

With uncertainty

And doubt

In your mind!

Like

South Africa

Today,

For lots,

Life now is not

So sweet,

They have

No other option

Than to act

With their feet!

Previously living

In a comfort zone,

Then moving and

All alone!

On arriving on

Foreign shore,

Knowing that

Your life,

Will not be,

The same

Anymore!

With hope

In your heart,

Wishes,

In your head,

Praying at night

While lying in bed!

Looking for work,

Sometimes,

You are skint,

Hoping to

Land a job

And make a mint!

Looking for soil,

To plant

Some new roots,

Gone are

The takkies

And flip flops,

Now wearing

Waterproof boots!

May you be fruitful

And prosperous,

Wherever

You land!

May the

Universal Spirit,

Guide you and

Hold your

Hand!

Hay!

"Make bread

While the oven is hot!"

As the bakers say!

Or is it?

"While the

Sun shines,

Make hay!"

Head!

Why is Brexit

Happening anyway?

Was it not due

To a split

In the Tory party?

Where some of the

Really rich ones

Didn't want any tax

To have to pay!

As the EU,

With

Tax havens

They were going

To do away!

They thought,

"No way!"

So, the question

Was put out

In a referendum,

"Do you want

To leave the EU?

Or do

You want to stay?"

Several politicians

With sparkles

In their eyes!

Then proceeded

To tell,

Just plain

Outright lies!

The vote

Was a very

Close run thing!

With many alarm bells,

Now beginning

Inside a lot of

Minds to ring!

Splitting the country

Down to the core!

With car manufacturers

And other

Businesses leaving,

Saying

"After Brexit

We cannot operate

In Britain anymore!"

This of course,

Will leave many

Thousands of families

Without an income

Any more!

The EU also wanted

To raise

The pension payout!

So that the elderly

In the UK would get

The same pension,

As pensioners in Europe,

But it being about

Three times as much,

This was questionably

By the government

In much doubt!

So, what started

As an internal division,

In the Tory party!

Will now lead many

People to grieve!

But there is more

Than a little

Sense of irony!

As the ones in the party!

Who wanted to leave!

Pay very little tax

You see!

So now we are in this fiasco

People wondering

What will happen?

As many have said,

And the government

Running around

Like a chicken

Without

A

Head!

26.03.2019

Here!

Friends

Often say

What

Another person,

Needs to hear!

Sometimes words,

From a stranger

Show you that,

The Spirit

Is

Here!

Him too!

So, I just get back

At three,

From a week's leave,

"Please phone Kristian,

Your agent!"

Is the message

That I did receive!

I wonder what's wrong?

That I could not see?

When an e mail arrives

From him to me!

He forwarded an e mail

From the man

Who runs the camp

Where I stay!

And this is what

He did say!

"I had a situation

With one

Of your workers

Today at breakfast,

He ended up

Shouting and swearing,

Not at all cool!

And said his name

Was David Nicoll

He might be taking

Us for a fool?"

"He was filling his

Water bottle

Inside the canteen!

It is against the rules

To do that,

Because of transfer

Of bacteria

From bottle to spout,

If you know what I mean?"

"I told him that

It is against the rules,

As my patience,

I swallowed!

Then told him,

These rules,

Must be followed!

He left his

Bottle outside,

As he left for work,

Not to be late!

But his anger

And verbal abuse

We just

Cannot tolerate!

I was called many things

Of which I do not

Wish to say!

Then told him,

You can

Drink the water

From the taps,

Here in Norway!

He does not

Come from here,

He is from

Some other nation!

He then threatened to

Sue me if he

Has an accident at work?

Due to dehydration!

He didn't want

To listen to me!

Just kept

Swearing and shouting

Profanity!

He is

Not welcome

To stay at

The camp anymore,

After work today,

He is out!

Forever more!"

Well, this came as a shock,

That much I can say!

So, I went to

The canteen office

Straight away!

"I believe

That you had a problem

This morning,

Sorry to hear about it,

It was not me,

That is not my game!

But it pisses me off,

That someone

Should use,

My name,

In vain!"

"It is OK David,

We know you,

And

That it

Was not you!"

"Well, please

Let me know

Who it was,

When you find out,

As I would like

To have,

A word

With him

Too!"

History!

What a great night last night!

Everything working out right!

Met Karim,

From Morocco on the street,

In Stavanger, Norway,

A couple of weeks ago!

He was carrying

A very small strange

Double ended drum,

"What is that?"

I wanted to know!

I have just come back

From South Africa

And love to play

The djembe drum!

Once you are into the rhythm,

See the atmosphere hum!

So, we exchange phone numbers,

Willingly!

And decide that in the future

Each other we should see!

That happened last night,

And it all worked out right!

He took me to a

Norwegian Professor's apartment,

Not far from the sea,

In Stavanger's CBD!

There was also a

Liberian man there,

With egg shakers,

Shaking them

Like a star,

With the Prof.

Playing acoustic,

Gut string guitar!

They were recording

Though an expensive

Hanging mike!

It sounded brilliant,

So different,

Had never

Heard the like!

Karim playing multi

Percussion,

Four instruments

At the same time!

Then I came in

With the steady

Djembe rhythm

And poetry in rhyme!

What a sound

And sight to see!

With backing

By Moroccan

And Liberian

Vocal harmony!

God willing,

We are going

To go far!

That much

I can see!

So, this Tuesday night

We are,

For the first time

Going to play

In a local

Stavanger bar

And create

Our own,

History!

Hit!

Witnessed an unpleasant

Situation last night,

Created by an

English workmate!

Who said something not right!

Sitting in the canteen

Having my evening meal,

Then got joined by a Scots friend

We were having good crack!

Talking without end,

Then an Englishman joins us,

"What are you doing here?"

Was the question

That my mate was asked,

This pissed him off,

You could see that,

His mind

Was no longer relaxed!

"I came to sit with my mate!"

Was his reply

"You don't have any!"

The protagonist did reply!

Well, this went from bad to worse!

Leaving me to inwardly curse!

Would have ended it

There and then if I could,

When the dude,

Who started all the shit,

Said to him

"You are rude!"

I asked him to chill out

And to sit back,

He told me to

"Stay out of it!"

Forcefully,

Not in good crack!

This put my mate

Right off his meal!

Can't blame him,

He was now

Irritated and angry!

Then he left the table

Holding his temper back

While he was still able!

"I am not going to let this go!"

Said the Englishman to me!

Then he followed him

Out of the canteen door!

So, the one

Who started all the shit,

Not in good crack or wit!

Better be careful

Behaving like that,

As one day

He might

Get hit!

Humanity!

Some people surely

Have a great

Sense of humour!

At least that is what I see!

For they are

Poisoning our air!

Beyond compare!

The long white lines

In the sky are there,

For all with eyes to see!

This is insanity!

If there is one thing,

That we all

Have in common,

The most

Common denominator,

That there can be!

We all need to

Breathe clean air,

And who are you

To do this to

All living things

As well as

ALL

Of

Humanity!

I Go!

To get to the camping ground

From the car park,

Looked like a bit of a slog!

About half a mile walk

And now some of the earth

Has turned into bog!

Didn't fancy carrying the tent,

Sleeping bag, inflatable mattress,

Backpack and cameras, you see!

So, came up with Plan B!

Had a hammock in the backpack

And hung it under a beautiful

Massive old Oak tree!

Such a cool position

With everyone walking by,

The evening Sun beaming down,

So peacefully!

Me thinking

For the night,

This'll do me!

Go to watch Lulu perform,

She is vibrant, full of fun!

Then return to the tree,

To find that

My hammock is gone!

Oh Lord, I didn't think

That it would get stolen,

An ashen look on my face!

Where under the

Leafy green branch,

There was now no hammock,

Only lots of space!

It was an interesting spot,

That much you will see,

As instead of standing

In long queues to use

The portable toilets,

Lots used to come

And fertilise the tree!

Men to the left,

Women to the right!

Under the green canopy,

A bit out of sight!

After this annual

Mass fertilisation,

This tree will grow!

Next year,

I will be back

With another hammock,

But will take it with me

Everywhere

I Go!

Immortalised!

Have I got news
For you Cameron,
This you will see!
As you are involved
In a wee bit of History,
Please check on KDP,
The latest book
Release by me,
Called David Nicoll,
Thoughts and Reflections
Vol 3!
Got this out
Very quickly
As I am sure that
This story
To your friends,
You will relate!
As it includes,
A photo of you
And the two ladies
Who were with us,
Which goes
With the poem
"Do you
Fancy me?
Or
My mate?"
Hot off the press!
Is what they say,
As this
Only happened
Last Sunday!
Once the
Paperback,
Comes out,
I am sure,
It will
Be prized,
The day
That you,
Were Immortalised!

"Do you fancy me or my mate?"

Insanity!

We see them from the ground,

In many global photo and video!

And Robert M Deutsch

From satellite views

The scale of this

Global insanity does show!

But many Homo Sapiens

Their existence they still deny,

When these

CHEMical TRAILS

Are there as plain as day,

Spreading over our,

Mother Earth's sky.

Spreading dis-ease

And poison

For the few to rule,

While treating

All of nature

With contempt

Like a fool.

But what good is

Dead money,

Locked up in a vault,

If the damage and waste

You cannot halt?

There is no doubt

As far as I can see,

That to play God

And change

The natural balance

Of our finely tuned

Weather

Covertly,

Is indeed

Insanity!

Irretrievably!

This is

An absolutely

Disgusting sight!

And before the

1930s

Was never seen,

It is not right!

Plastic pollution,

Of the land,

Air and sea,

Is created easily!

Before that time,

There were

No plastics

You see!

But then

They banned Hemp,

Please Google

The Hemp story!

As since then,

We have polluted

The world

In some cases

Irretrievably!

It!

A new type

Of weather

Forecasting,

Takes place

Today,

I say this

Using some

Wit!

First,

You

Forecast it!

Then you

Create

It!

Key!

Was just thinking,

To be true activists,

We could copy,

Extinction Rebellion,

So easily!

Block

Off a road!

Then get

Locked up,

With

No

Press coverage,

Then they

Might even,

Throw

Away

The

Key!

Lawyer!

We all have

To do something

To earn

Our bread!

"What is

Black and brown

And looks

Good on

A lawyer?"

"A Rottweiler!"

He said!

Leg up!

Met up with Jamie Houston

Of Creative Scotland

Last Wednesday

Everything went very well,

That I must say!

As they can help you

To make your artistic dreams

And thoughts to achievement,

Come true!

This for me is already

A dream come true!

So now imagination,

Is the only limitation

And drip by drip

We will fill the cup!

When the time is right Jamie

We can meet again

And I will give you

All you need

To give me a

Leg up!

Material!

So,

I am standing

In the lift

At work,

With Murdo,

My pal!

When this

Gorgeous,

Slinky,

Blonde lady

Comes in,

Me thinking,

Man,

She is

Marriage

Material!

Me!

My baby

Was not happy!

That much

I could see!

Then she said

"This morning

When you woke,

You were

More

Interested

In

Facebook,

Than

Me!

Memory!

"A random question."

He said

Asked by my son Paul,

In a Facebook message,

"What did your father do

For work

When he was here

In a previous age?"

"He was a carpenter

To start with!"

I replied,

"But why

Do you ask me

That question?"

It seemed strange!

"I saw the name

Peter Nicoll,

In a post in

Stornoway

Now and then!

Today!"

Is what he did say!

He then

Sent me the photo,

Which brought tears

To my eyes,

And got me

Very emotional,

Quietly heaving,

With tears flowing

And sighs!

Wiping them away,

Trying to not let others

In the office see!

My emotions,

Now running free!

"Yes, that is him

On the right!"

He was young then

And before,

This photo

I never did see!

My,

How a photo

Can bring back

Many a

Memory!

Mercury!

As if we don't have

Enough on our minds,

What with long white

Trails all over our skies

For all to see!

Fluoride in our water,

GMOs in our food,

And soon mm

Microwave 5G!

Don't mean to trouble

You with this,

But it is another,

Vapours from

Teeth fillings

Of

Mercury!

Move!

Three things

To keep

Private,

To keep

You free

And in

The groove!

Your

Love life!

Your

Income

And

Your

Next

Move!

My Leg!

Was in bed

With a blind

Lady last night!

Met her

At the Keg!

She said,

"I had the

Biggest penis,

That she

Had ever felt!"

I told her!

"You are

Pulling

My leg!"

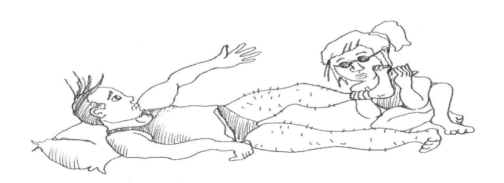

NoScabangosInStavanga!

It started with Karim, Stan

And the Liberian man!

Then along came

Rob and me!

We are now all

Playing together,

In rhythm, melody

And harmony!

What is the future?

Well, we shall see!

As we create our own

History!

A real

Ethnic mix,

In Norwegian land,

From

Morocco,

South Africa,

Liberia,

Norway,

Albania

And

Scotland!

All living free,

With a

Desire to be,

Whatever our heart,

Aspires!

With multifaceted

Percussion,

Sure, to light

Some fires!

Sometimes playing

African and

Latin American rhythms

Shaking the Tanga!

And noticing that

There are

NoScabangosInStavanga!*

*= Thief in South Africa!

Not On!

This protest march,

Is about

Lions in captivity!

They are bred

In enclosures!

Kept well away,

From other men's activity!

Really not much of a life,

Bred like cattle in a pen!

No thought for their

Spirits and souls,

Used to be called

The King of beasts!

Way back when!

Day in, day out,

Crammed in

An enclosure,

Nowhere to hunt,

Roam or see!

Jailed by man,

Bred to die!

A lucrative

Business you see!

With less Lions

In the wild now,

Than in captivity!

New blood taken in

From time to time,

Fresh from the wild!

To inject new genes,

To the unborn child!

The purpose is twofold!

The Lion will

Die on a game farm,

By either bullet or bow!

Bought at a price,

Between buyer and seller,

Which would be

Interesting to know!

After that

It will be skinned,

Made into a mount,

Rug or trophy!

Flown overseas,

Via the Taxidermist,

For the hunters

Friends and family to see!

Along with,

The obligatory photo,

Rifle in hand,

Having killed a wild lion,

In the

Wilds of Africa you see!

This is hypocrisy!

So, then that

Leaves the corpses,

De skinned,

Some beheaded,

Just muscle and bone!

They are in demand!

Used to make

Tiger bone wine

In eastern Asian land!

So, the breeders are

Making a killing,

In more ways than one!

It's just that for

The proud Lions

It is not much fun!

Is this going to be,

Allowed to carry on?

It is,

Not on!

Not on!

Not on!

Not See!

This is so close

To the truth

In Scotland

Unfortunately,

As a lot

Of people

There,

Just

Do

Not

See!

Now!

Now!

Is the time,

To live life!

Enjoy

And

Have fun!

As

One day,

You

Will be

Gone!

Of it!

Sleeping in the car

Eating on the run!

Selling possessions

For little cash

Sometimes stressful

Sometimes OK!

Sometimes not fun!

Situations in life

That one goes through,

Got myself into it!

Due to no job

For eleven months,

Spending all my saved cash

And now temporarily

In the shit!

But God willing

He will help us

To get out

Of it!

Omnicide!

Some take life

For what it

Has to offer,

They live it to the full,

Take it for a ride!

Some others,

Through circumstances,

Situations and outlooks,

They commit suicide!

Some other people,

Tribes or nations

Also, for power,

Land, water, oil,

Or other resources?

On others,

They

Commit genocide!

With all the poisoning

Of our beautiful home,

In one form or another

Nowadays,

It

Can only

Be described

As

Omnicide!

Oran mor!

Said to my son Mark
Having just come back
To Scotland for
The Xmas holiday.
That out one night
We should go and let
Our Spirits play!
He said "OK!"
"Well actually
After thinking about it
I think that
We should go to church!"
He looked distraught!
Kind of awkwardly
Left in the lurch!
Didn't really need
Any more to say,
So, told him,
"Son, I want to
Take you somewhere
That you will remember
Forever more!
We shall go to
Oran mor!"

Out!

There is
Something
Very poetic
About this
Photograph,
From what
I can see!
The Sea
Is just like,
Our human
Body!
If bad stuff
Gets put in,
You feel sick,
Without
A doubt!
And when
Your body,
Cannot
Handle it
Anymore,
It
Pukes
The lot
Out!

Pal!

Taking photos

Of a lady's tattoo,

As I do!

She said

I have a friend

Who has some too!

Her photo

Is in my phone,

She is single,

All alone!

She is quite a gal!"

She then

Showed me

Her friends'

Photo,

Told her,

"I think

I need to meet

Your

Pal!"

Pay!

What is going on

Nowadays on Facebook?

Getting friend requests,

From all over the world

From people that

Presumably at my wall,

Would like to look?

Really don't know?

It is difficult to say!

But thinking that

Some of them,

Are trying

To get some pay!

Are you in a relationship?

The one lady asked of me,

But to be honest,

You are communicating

With a photograph,

Of the person,

That you are

Talking to

Hopefully,

But of that,

There is no

Certainty!

Then she says

"Would you like

A relationship with me?"

"But you are in the USA,

Between us is,

A big sea!"

"Just give me

Your phone number!"

She asked

Quite eloquently!

Well the thought

Of giving

Out my number

Made me wail!

Thinking,

Is she into

Some form of

On air,

Commercial

Wholesale!

People will

Try anything,

New scams

Always on the go!

And if you

Haven't been

Stung with it before,

Then soon,

You will know!

So never mind the

Relationship lady,

I will rather just

Go with

The flow!

Then thought

OK, give her

Your number,

Let's see

What she will do?

Then get a message

"Send me back the code,

Now!

Urgently

As this code,

I need to know!"

It was a code

To reset my

Facebook password

Then I thought

No!!!

She, or he?

Was persistent

Egging me on,

Saying

"I need

This code urgently!"

Turning out

That our interchange

Was not after all

So much fun!

You must

Be very careful

In the world today

As some try

To genuinely

Help you,

But the rest

Want to get,

Out of you

Some

Cash,

Extortion,

Blackmail

Or

Pay!

Planting!

Been
Digging holes
For the
Whole day!
To make
Things worse
The day,
Was
Monday!
My hands
Are sore,
My back
It aches!
But to
Grow
Some food
In Kenya,
We do,
What it
Takes!
There is
No good,
In raving
And
Ranting!
All that is
Left now
Is
The
Planting!

Poetry!

Handing out flyers with

My website address,

Published books and CDs on,

To get the word out,

Has sure been fun!

Basically, giving them,

To whoever that I talked to,

Some poetry,

Some with illustrations,

Some with matching photographs

And some

With music too!

Seemed like a great idea

And to get the word out,

A great thing to do!

Quite a selection of poetry!

With many varied styles of music,

On David Nicoll and friends

Vols. 1,2 and 3!

Recorded and produced

In South Africa

By many great friends/musicians

And me!

Then a rocking, reggae, soul,

Easy listening experience,

On the six MAD,

Mervyn and Dave CDs

Containing lyrics which will

Hopefully make

A real difference!

If people just listen

To the songs with titles,

With which they resonate,

Could be valuable information

Which makes a lot of sense!

With which they

Could relate!

Hold on tight and

Don't give up

Are only two,

Thanks! and

A little bit of sunshine,

Could easily get to you!

Then there is the book

Showing photographs

Of many a South African tattoo!

The books,

Thoughts and Reflections

Vols. 1, 2 and 3!

Are all filled with many various

Forms, styles and subjects

For poetry,

From wildlife to environmental,

Humanitarian with some

To make you laugh or smile,

Others are thought provoking,

To make you think of something,

That you haven't thought,

If indeed you ever have?

For quite a while!

Easy flowing,

You know the score,

Maybe some will make you think

In ways that you

Have not thought before?

They are all released

In the same way,

With the initial release,

Having the photographs

In black and white

For those who don't want

So much to pay!

Each book has now been revised,

Which makes a real difference

On the run!

As the full colour photographs

Are all in the book titles,

Followed by (Rev 1)

Then there are

The books of POKES!

Some with great illustrations,

They are POetic joKES!

If you have a sense of humour,

You will really love these!

As they will make you laugh

And put your mind at ease!

The Poetic Picture books

Are pleasing to see!

With great photographs

And on top of them,

Matching POKEs

(POetic joKEs)

And poetry!

On the website

www.davidnicoll.co.uk

Are also performance videos,

Of myself and others!

Like Jim Ferguson,

Oliver Pissed,

Billy Bonkers,

Hybrid 21 and others!

All great Scottish poets

And genuine brothers!

There is also

A section for tattoos

And Body Art!

Collected in my travels,

An ongoing project in

The Northern Hemisphere

And fun right from the start!

Wherever I am,

Wherever I go!

If I see someone with

Tattoos I ask them,

Can I possibly

Photograph them?

Ever so slow!

Most say "Yes!"

But some say "No!"

What a selection,

For everyone to see,

What people do

To permanently,

Adorn

The skin of their body!

Everyone is unique,

In the choices they make,

What tattoos they choose?

And where

They choose to put them,

Make no mistake!

Capturing mobile 3D art

From the start,

Has always been my game!

Both men and women,

Doing their own thing

And no two on the earth

Are the same!

Then there is the link

To the SMAAPP page!

Scottish Musicians and Artistes

Against the Poisoning

Of our Planet,

Is in a growth stage,

As we have many potential

Hazards in this day and age!

The website created

By my son Mark and me,

In our creative hub

In Crow road,

Glasgow!

Him designing T shirts,

Me doing my own thing

For the world to see!

Then a thought,

Came to me!

Passing through Amsterdam

Airport on my way

To and from Stavanger

As I do!

Bought big packets

Of Danish bulbs,

To let some beauty,

Shine through!

Various flowers,

Of different type

And colour hue!

I got envelopes,

Then put a mixture of three

In each with the flyer,

Seems like a great thing

To do!

It is appreciated,

That much I can see,

When people ask

"What are they for?"

I tell them

"To bring into your life

Some growth and beauty!"

"Just get a pot,

Some potting soil,

You can involve

Your son or daughter!

Then once a fortnight

Just give them

Some water!"

"I love it!"

Was the one reply,

From a young lady,

Who you could see,

It made her

Spirit fly!

To give growth and beauty,

In a world

Full of indifference,

Coldness, isolation

And ignominy!

To give them something

For their eyes,

Heart

And Soul to be

Set free,

Which,

After all

In itself

Is

Poetry!

Prevail!

It was on the

American news

Not too long ago,

There are now

Twelve

New classifications

Of clouds that on

The wind they flow!

Asperitas, Murus

And Volutus too!

Three strange new

Phenomenon

Have now come

Into view!

Where did they come from?

From where did they appear?

For many billions of years

Of the earth's evolution

They were neither

Far nor near!

They just were not here!

Listed in the

International Cloud Atlas

With photos as well!

But as to where

Did they come from?

No one asks,

None will tell!

Well, they started

Their existence

In many a chemical drum!

Filled with Nano particulates

Of Aluminium, Barium

And Strontium!

Then through

Either winter

Or summer,

Daytime or night!

They were released

Through spray nozzles

From Aeroplanes,

Leaving in the sky

A strange sight!

For how long

Has Humanity

Seen them globally?

The long white streaks

Lingering in the sky!

Spread by nameless

Unidentified aircraft

Flying way up high!

But people live

Just day by day!

Not noticing or caring

Either way!

And they

Don't want to know,

Some of them

When you have something

About them to say!

There are only

Ten basic

Cloud genera,

Now there are

Twelve more!

Supposed to have come from

The ten but that is Bullshit!

The enlightened ones

Know the score!

They look

So amazing in sunsets

Beautiful colours

In sunshine or rain!

But unknowingly

Most of these clouds

Are bringing many a Dis-ease,

Poisoning and imbalance,

In fact, they

Are on natures balance,

Creating real strain!

Now some of these clouds

After spreading

Look wispy like sails!

Their father or creator

For many of them actually

Is what is known

As Chemtrails!

But very few believe this

As Chemtrails

Are listed as

A conspiracy!

To keep the masses

Ignorant of the truth,

The reality!

Most people are too busy

With Sport, Cell phones

Computers and TV!

Admiring the beautiful sunsets

Without realizing the danger,

Or not listening

To knowledge given freely

By a stranger!

But stop they must!

And stop they will!

For the ultimate plan

Is for many billions

To kill!

This is a truth

Clearly stated!

That with nearly

Eight billion people

On this planet,

It is now

Overpopulated!

Such madness

And on such

A great scale!

Many brain and respiratory

Infections will leave

Many to groan and wail!

It will undoubtedly

Leave many with a frown!

Please realize

That if something is

Aerosolized in the sky above you,

Then ultimately it will

Fall down!

These Nano particles

Cause chest infections,

The Aluminium

Goes into the blood

Via the lungs

And then into the brain!

Creating many unwanted

Deadly Dis-eases

And creating for you,

Your children,

Grandchildren,

Neighbours and friends

Lots and lots of strain!

The only way out of this

Is by global mass unity

Or Homo sapiens

As we know them

Will be a very sad tale!

If billions of people

Around the planet

Don't wake up

And join up,

How is

Good ever

Going to

Prevail?

Rain!

Never seen

Such a

Happy man,

Begging

In the street,

Just above

Waverly station

In Edinburgh,

Passers by

Giving him food,

Which was really

Very neat!

This man,

Was

Obviously

Feeling

No strain!

Sitting,

Smiling,

Eating,

In the

Rain!

RAIN!

This photo shatters
Two commonly held beliefs.

"You cannot build
Using these stones."

That comment
Caused me strain.

The other was,
"You cannot
Photograph
Rain!"

Reality!

A martyr,

A martyr,

I don't want

To be!

Only to

Wake

Peoples

Minds

Up,

To

Reality!

Regret!

I call them

Long white streaks

In the sky!

As the word Chemtrails

Is looked on as a conspiracy,

Even though these

Sun blocking,

Spreading streaks,

Criss cross our skies,

For those with eyes to see!

Some leaving almost

Unnatural colours in

Sunrise and Sunset,

Have seen videos of

The sprays being

Switched on and off,

So, it's not caused

By wing tip vortices,

When the

Atmosphere is wet!

It is an assault on

Humanity and

All living life forms

On this

Glorious planet,

Much to my

Regret!

Rent!

Got a bit of a

Shock last night!

My lady video called

On Facebook messenger,

She was looking alright!

Had jewels round her neck,

A tiara in her hair,

Looking better

Than she had in ages,

No longer in despair!

Almost exactly

A year ago,

That I had to

Leave her there!

The first thing

That I did see!

Is that she now

Has a place,

Right

Next to the sea!

In a big block

Of fancy holiday flats,

That are known to me!

She seemed very happy!

She's had a tough time

Since I left,

Leaving her bereft,

Stuck in Mossel bay!

A lovely place

I must say,

But not too great

If you have no job

And are not receiving

Any pay!

I wish her health,

I wish her power!

Wonder if she

Remembers,

The spot

In front of her,

Where we used to

Be forced to

Have a

Cold water shower?

Helped by a man

Who owns most

Of the town!

He wanted her badly

When I had her,

No doubt

At that time,

Leaving him

With a frown!

But time passes,

Things change,

It's not

So strange!

It's as if,

It was

Almost meant!

Just wondering

To myself,

A little

Question,

How,

Is she

Going to

Pay

The

Rent?

Rhino!

I say,

Poison the horn

Of every single

Living Rhino!

Drill them

Criss cross,

Put in poison!

Then the users,

Will soon

Get to know!

That it is

Not very cool,

Or advisable,

For

Health reasons,

To use

The horn

Anymore,

From any

Rhino!

Ride!

I am walking

Along the pavement

And then,

Moved to the side,

Saw a cyclist

Coming along,

With something

In a basket

At his front side!

Looks like

He doesn't

Take his

Dog for a walk,

But

Instead,

Takes him

For a

Ride!

Right!

Hi Johnny boy,

I write you this

In pain!

Looks like

I need to

Come and see

You again!

My saliva glands

Are sore,

Can't eat

Properly

No more!

To put it

Bluntly,

My mouth

Is sore!

Should

Have actually,

Come and seen you,

The very next day,

As now,

I am back

In Stavanger,

Norway!

Will be back

In Scotland,

Next Tuesday

And then

We must

Get it right!

As I have

A book launch on

That very night

And must

Be able

To speak

Right!

Salesman!

Never been one

To be without

A plan,

Now,

I am

A poetry

Book

Salesman!

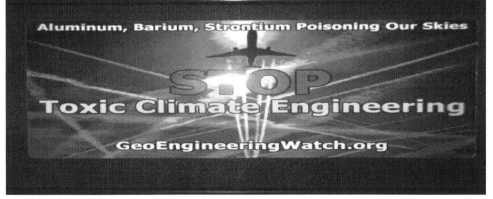

Saturday!

Now started work

In Stavanger, Norway!

Beautiful city

That much I can say!

Picked up some

Ornithological habits,

As I go

Birdwatching

In town

Every

Saturday!

Save!

So,

Some Harvard

University academics,

And the global ruling elite,

Have decided in their wisdom,

A way to sort this out,

Is to block the Sun!

This is happening everywhere

From the ground and satellite

We see it all over,

From Australia, China,

Africa, America,

Europe and even

The white cliffs of Dover!

It is causing death,

It is causing Dis-Ease!

With the majority

Of humanity,

Not being able to see,

The wood from the trees!

In a very short space

Of Universal time,

We have taken this

Pristine blue jewel,

With its natural balance,

Of nature in harmony!

To almost a point

Of no return,

Although this fact

Not many see!

So many

Problems and situations,

On the planet today!

From deforestation,

Species extinction,

Plastic pollution,

Forced vaccinations

And now 5G!

What will our future be?

What an absolute

Cock up we have made,

Of our custody!

Of the only habitable planet

That we know of,

Or can see!

Nature will strike back!

Of that you can be sure!

It does not sit on the fence,

For every action,

There is an equal and opposite

Reaction,

Although not that many

Can see this sense!

The curse of Homo Sapiens,

On whatever

He does feed!

Was his invention

Of a thing called Money,

And a feeling

Known as Greed!

But what good

Is all your money?

If this planet

We cannot save!

You cannot

And will not,

Take any of your money

To your grave!

Dear God and

Universal Spirit!

Guide and help us,

So that,

Our Mother Earth

And all her

Lifeforms,

We can

Save!

Saw the Sun!

Saw

The Sun

Coming up

This morning

Going to be

A beautiful

Sunny day!

An hour later,

I went out and saw

In the skies they were

Beginning to spray!

Then the

White lines spread out,

Across the sky,

As the haze takes over

Hazing the sky!

They are

Changing our weather,

Without a doubt!

As if they had not

Sprayed today,

Then the sun

Would be full out!

But now it is

Diffused

Without a doubt!

Less sunshine

Coming through

Is not good

For man nor beast!

As our

Food production

Will be lower,

Gone will

Be the days

For some,

Of the

Feast!

See!

In this cave
There is a story
Of Humanity!
And some
Of our ancient
History,
It is near,
Mossel bay in
South Africa
And is known
As cave 13b,
People lived
In this cave
Over 160,000
Years ago,
When nature ruled
And the seasons
Passed slow!
They used
It for shelter,
To live in,
Cook, eat
And breed!
Scavenging
The shores
And hunting
To supply
Their need!
At that time,
The sea
Was over five
Kilometres away,
There were only about
Five thousand people
On the planet
At that time,
Which just
Goes to show!
That we all
Have common
Ancestors!
Evolving equivalent
To the way all
Modern dogs did,
From the Wolf,

Gradually and slow!
Into many races
With different,
Features,
Skin colours,
Sizes, shapes
And faces!
Excavations in the cave
Unearthed ancient stone
Cutting and grinding tools,
Animal bones, shellfish,
Survival was the only
Concern in these days,
They were not fools!
Inside, they would cook
And stay warm,
Sheltering from
Blistering sunshine,
Or any
Pervasive storm!
Tucked in the base of
A massive rock wall,
These hunter gatherers
Were not so tall!
An amazing place
For Archaeology!
To see the views,
That you Ancestors
Used to see!
Pristine in its time,
A pleasure to see!
Unpolluted,
Without plastics,
Toxic by-products,
Or mm microwaves,
From the
New phenomenon
Known as 5G,
The Point of
Human Origins
Is indeed a place
That
You
Should
Most
Definitely
See!

Mossel Bay, South Africa

160 000 years ago

2019

www.humanorigin.co.za

Seen!

Since I started working

In Stavanger, Norway

I have taken an interest

In Ornithology!

As each Saturday night

I go out to town,

And see how many

Beautiful Birds,

That I can see!

Just last night

While walking down the street,

These fine Birds

I happened to meet!

They were getting photos taken

With friends and many a fan!

As they are showgirls,

Then the one who was

A real nice lady said

"I want a photograph

With this man!"

Something said to me,

Hold on,

As the hairs

On my arms did creep!

As a couple of them

Had voices

That were quite deep!

Looking for bulges

In the crotch

But none to be seen,

Me thinking,

Is there more

Than one drag queen?

But it was all in good fun

And a sight to be

Seen!

Sing!

A lovely comment that you

Make there Mim!

And every word is true!

Now you are about to go

On your yearly migration

As some other feathered

Birds do!

The beauty of this

Has a certain ring!

The reason that

You are flying

Is symbiotic

With them,

As when

You arrive

You will

Sing!

Written for Miriam Erasmus who flies from South Africa

To the UK every summer to play guitar and sing her songs.

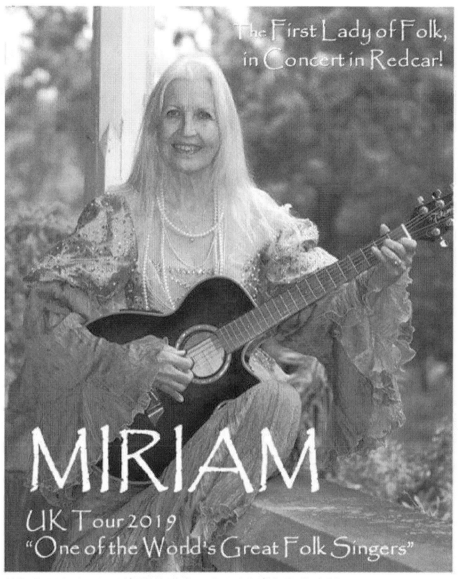

The First Lady of Folk, in Concert in Redcar!

MIRIAM

UK Tour 2019
"One of the World's Great Folk Singers"

Miriam Erasmus (Miriam Backhouse) in Concert
Featuring Maggie Gee, your MC for the evening

CLAXTON HOTEL, REDCAR TS10 3AW

Wednesday 14th August 2019 from 7.30pm

Doors open 7.00pm – price £5.00 on the door
Proceeds donated to Zetland Lifeboat Museum, Redcar

Sheets!

"I like to

Leave my mark!"

She said,

While chewing on

Some sweets!

"Where did

I leave it here?"

She asked,

I replied,

"On the

Sheets!"

Sky!

It's

Almost

Enough

To make

You cry!

These

Anonymous

Planes

That are

Painting

Our

Sky!

Sow!

It's taken
A bit of time,
A lot of effort
With creativity,
Flowing free!
Capturing moments,
In rhythm,
Metre and rhyme!
Embellishing
The initial thought,
Value adding,
With music,
With illustrations,
With lyric video,
The results
Sublime!
Food for thought!
Or a POKE
POetic joKE,
To laugh
And smile!
Or think about
Humanity,
Wildlife
And
Ecology,
Once in
A while!

But as they say,

As we all know!

You reap,

What you

Sow!

Spray!

A question!

It came to me last night,

While lying in my bed!

To ALL the environmental

Groups in the world,

Why is it that

Coal fly ash,

Is captured at

Power stations

And not allowed

To escape to

Float over our head?

Is it because

It is, Poisonous and toxic?

That it would make

The population,

Sick or dead?

You know that this is true!

As well as I do!

That is why we have

Environmental

Laws against this,

That is what I say,

Then why do you

Allow planes,

In our skies

This same toxic mix

To spray?

Sprays!

Lovely sunny evening

In Norway yesterday!

The skies were

Blue and clear!

So, I decided

To go fishing.

As the sea it is

Quite near!

Across by the

Mound of boulders

Setting up the fishing line,

At one with nature

And feeling fine!

Then look up in the sky

And what do I see?

Planes spraying

Long white

Spreading trails,

In number,

There were three!

This is now,

Creating in me,

Disharmony!

The speedboats

Moving quickly,

Very fast!

The people onboard,

No doubt having

A blast!

And the sky,

Now upon waking

In the morning,

Is now

Completely grey

And overcast!

Now it is

Midsummer,

The grass is

Very green!

Did they notice

The cross in the sky

Above them?

But no doubt for them,

It was completely

Unseen!

Taken as normal

Everywhere nowadays!

These overhead,

Coal fly ash,

Poisonous

And toxic,

Sprays!

Stars!

One aged

Seventy-four,

The other

Sixty-five,

Both

Loving life,

Scottish

Performance

Poets/Percussionists,

Both glad

To be

Still alive!

Loving

Live music,

In the

Scotia and Clutha

Glaswegian bars,

Listening to

All

The

Established

And

Up

And

Coming

Stars!

Bert Stables and David Nicoll

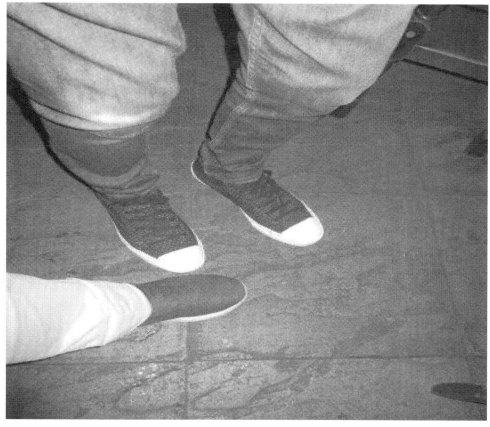

Synchronicity!

What a brilliant
Night last night!
A real joyful story!
Went and performed
In Stavanger at Osterwag 41,
Blyge Harry!
The music
Was brilliant,
The people all happy,
Energized, motivated
And free!
Karim, Stan and the
Liberian man,
Playing along with me!
Playing together
For the first time,
Creating our own history!
With gut string
Acoustic guitar,
Assorted percussion,
Djembe drum
And poetry!
Where this all leads?
We shall see!
Brought together
By chance,
Circumstance?
Or Synchronicity?

Tattoos!

In Life,

Sometimes,

You are happy!

Sometimes,

You have the Blues!

Sometimes,

You want To Be

Unique,

So, You Get

Yourself

Tattoos!

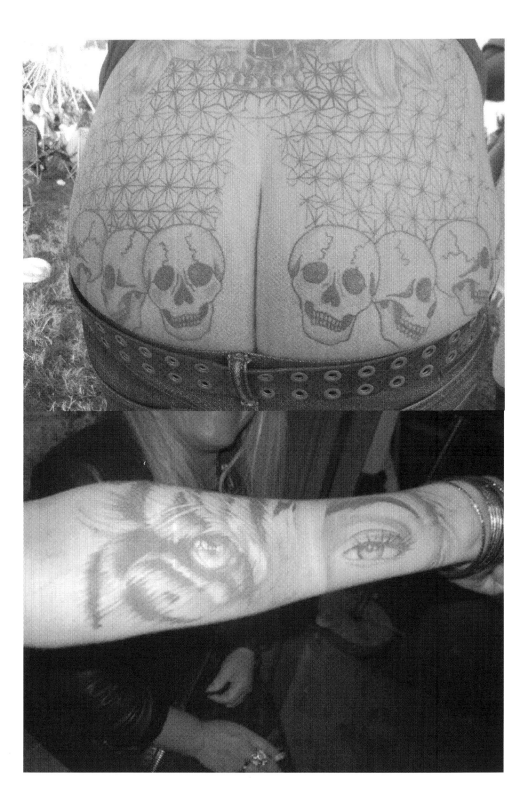

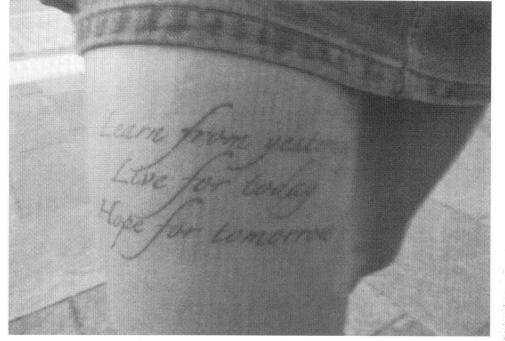

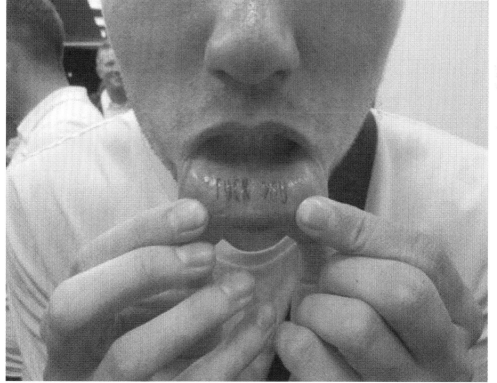

Technology!

For the first time

In eight months

My mind is at total peace!

No tinnitus,

Ringing in my ears,

Leaving my brain needing

No release!

At the top of Ben Nevis,

Where the air

Is crisp and clear!

Leaving me with a smile

And in good cheer!

I hope that this will last,

Don't know if it will,

Shall have to

Wait and see!

On returning

To Glasgow city!

With its

Recently switched on

mm wave 5G,

Technology!

The Blues!

Got told this

In Glasgow,

By a homeless man,

Who begs outside

A local restaurant,

Trying to

Make a plan!

"False beggars

Are on the street,

It's not too sweet,

They cover

Themselves in

A blanket and beanie,

As if they have nothing

To lose!

But the blanket

Covers up,

Their neat

Track suits

And two hundred

Pound shoes!

They take

The real

Homelesses

Earnings

Which

Gives me

The Blues!"

The day!

Follow on poem to
Him too!

Well, well,
How funny life can be!
As this morning,
Mick, he said to me!
"I found out who
Said he was you,
This is true!"
"I was standing outside
The TV room last night
Just having a smoke,
When this guy passes
Below me
And then talks
To another bloke!"
Who he was,
He did not know
And before
He had not seen!
Then the one
Tells the other
How he had
Had hassles,
That morning,
In the canteen!

He said that

He was arguing,

To this person that

He had just met

And had

Lost it completely

When the

Canteen manager

Told him that he could

Drink water

From his toilet!

Who he is?

Is the information

That I seek,

Just wondering,

Was the guy

That I photographed

His tattoos

Just last week?

It might well be,

We shall see,

It should not

Be so hard,

As he would

Have my name,

In his mind

As he would have

Seen it on

My business card!

Met him

In the corridor

When I came back

Just yesterday

Then he told me,

How he was

"Looking forward

To tomorrow

As to his home,

He was

Going away!"

This gets interesting,

That much

I can say!

Let's see

What develops

Through

The rest of

The day!

Thehardbard!

Stranding outside

The Scotia in Glasgow,

The oldest bar in town!

Happy with life,

Having a smoke,

Feeling high,

Not down!

Along comes a poet,

That I had met before!

He performed

At the first

SMAAPP LIVE

Awareness gig

At the Clutha,

Since then

Hadn't seen him

Any more!

This man is

Lots of fun,

His name is

Hybrid 21!

A colourful character,

Soft heart

Not hard!

So here are

Hybrid 21

And Thehardbard!

The summer!

Oh God!

The alarm clock

In the early morning,

Half past six

Comes by so quickly,

Without any warning!

Not even as if

You were on the booze!

It's just cold

And dark outside

So, you hit the button

Called snooze!

What the hell,

Stay in bed a bit longer,

Nothing to lose!

Apart from money,

Sleeping alone,

With no honey!

This getting up,

Early in the winter

Is a real bummer!

Roll on the summer!

Them!

A nugget

Of wisdom,

Now this

Is a Gem!

I get

Crazy

Ideas,

Then,

I do

Them!

Written about Saddam Hussein!

At the time of the first and second Gulf wars!

The Wild Arab!   **(To The tune of The Wild Rover!)**

He`s been a Wild Arab

For many`s a year

And he gassed Kurdish subjects

Just to make this clear!

He sent his army to

Kuwait by the sea!

Then he shot all the Generals

That didn't agree!

Chorus:

But its

Crude oil forever

Petrol, plastic and soap,

Crimplene and cosmetic's

All come from the gulf!

It's the first armchair war

That this worlds ever seen,

With CNN showing

It all on the screen,

When the allies they started

Their land war attack,

Holy Camel, said Saddam,

I'm pushing off back!

He's still now in power

A bit of a farce,

But very shortly

He'll no doubt be

Seeing his arse!

For the armies that are on

Your borders today,

Are very shortly

Going to take

Your freedom away!

Because its

Crude oil forever,

Petrol, plastic and soap,

Crimplene and cosmetic's

All come from the gulf!

Thistle!

Had a strange request,

That much is true!

My Swedish friend

Bamse,

Asked me

To design him,

A tattoo!

He is a massive man,

Not one,

That you would want

To fight!

Covered in tattoos,

With a big bushy beard,

That is pure white!

"Tell me some words

Of what you think

Of me!

Then put in some symbol

From your home country!"

Well, this got me thinking

It was quite hard,

So, I combined his name

With mine,

As I am known as

Thehardbard!

Haven't heard him sing

But heard him whistle,

So, topped it off

With the

Thehardbard

A	a	a
L	n	m
L	d	s
	s	e
	o	
	m	
	e	

To Me!

"The microchip

Has made a mockery

Of education!"

Bert said to me!

"As People

On The internet

No longer

Write,

Or spell

Properly!

So used to

Abbreviating

Every word

That they see!

They wont

Get a job

So easily!

Which makes

A mockery

Of

Education

To me!"

There!

Five artificial islands
Built in Lochs
In The Outer Hebrides
Over five thousand
Years ago!
Still there to this day,
Through
Summers heat
And winters snow!
Each with
A submerged
Walkway!
They range in size
From thirty,
To one hundred
Feet in diameter,
From Neolithic times,
Originally with
Round homes
Built over the water
In ancient times!
Ceramics have
Been found
In the waters,
Which have been
Radiocarbon dated,
From 3360 to 3640 BC
The reports stated!
Were they for religious,

Or funeral rituals?

Or possibly for feasts?

To move so

Many big stones

To build these things,

Some men,

Must have been

Strong as beasts!

Only questions remain

For the moment,

With no

Sure answers

To be fair,

For those that

Are interested,

The Crannogs

Are still

There!

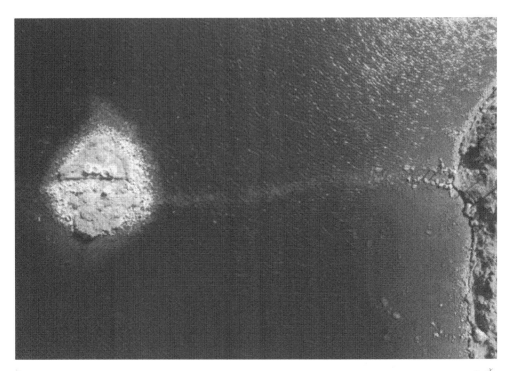

Three!

In Norway now,

It's the

Summer solstice,

But summer

Hasn't started,

As far as

I can see!

Reminds me of

Some previous

Hebridean

Summers,

Where they

Would start

At twelve

And finish

At

Three!

To see!

What a situation I now find myself in!

Not been eating so much, now getting thin!

Been in Knysna for eleven months now,

Haven't been able to find a job!

Used all my resources and funds up

Now in debt but was never one to rob!

Sitting in my old red Mercedes

Next to the road by the lagoon

With a "For Sale!"

Sign on the windscreen

Really hoping that someone

Will buy it real soon!

Need to make a break away

To get a job and earn

As this economy is depressed,

So, the many, many millions

Of unemployed people here learn!

Need to buy a

One-way ticket to Scotland

With my oldest son to stay!

Get a job as a

Senior piping designer there,

Pay my debts and save

To take this

Stress and depression away!

My lady and I need to leave

Our accommodation next Tuesday!

The heat is on, the pressure too

As we don't know yet

Where we will stay

In our old hometown

Of Mossel bay!

But we have both been praying

That God will show us the way!

Helped by a couple of friends

Angels without a doubt!

Going out of their way

To help us out!

"God bless you!" I shout!

Looking forward to

Coming back here sometime!

As overseas I will continue

To perform my poetry

In rhythm, metre and rhyme!

Promote my CDs and books,

Get more lyric videos done!

Help the animals,

People and environment

And have fun!

Most importantly

I am going to come back

For my young lady to see!

To see!.... Song lyrics

Ch..trails in the morning!

Ch..trails in the evening!

Cj..trails at suppertime!

Since they

Started spreading

Ch..trails

Their now

At it

All the time!

I wanted to

Print the full word,

But could not

You see!

Because if I had,

People would have said

This it is

A CONSPIRACY!

But it is not,

Is it

As these

Long white streaks

In the sky

Are there!

Plain as can be!

For all those

With eyes

To see!

To see!(3)

Now moved into

The twentieth century!

No more folded up

Pieces of paper,

But business cards

To hand out,

For other's

To see!

Today!

A moment for reflection,

Just came to me,

As exactly one year ago,

I was living in Lake Brenton

On the Knysna lagoon,

In South Africa,

Very close to the sea!

Beautiful place,

Where all the animals

Buck, birds and snakes,

Lived happy and free!

Naturally!

Peaceful it was,

There as if,

Heaven sent!

At a stage in my life

Where I

Was practising

Retirement!

Would get up

About nine

Feeling fine,

With very little strain!

Nothing to do,

No job to go to!

So, I would just

Go back to bed again!

With the love of my life,

Although she

Was not my wife,

Making love any time

Of the day!

Going to the

Golden beaches

And mountains

To take in the

Fresh air and peace,

While the time,

Whittled away!

Lighting fires

In the evening

While the air was still!

Cooking meat and fish,

On the barbeque,

(Braai) grill,

Drinking wine,

Feeling fine,

Sometimes,

The djembe drum

I would play,

But as in life,

Nothing is permanent,

Though you think

That it is at the time!

As the minutes, hours

And days pass away!

Then the money

Starts to run out

Creating strain,

In my mind

Without a doubt!

Looking for work,

But the

Economy was down!

And affirmative action

And BEE,

Meant I

Was unemployable,

No work

In this country

Or town!

Going down!

Still socially

It

Was fine as can be,

With friends in Knysna,

There were many!

Started a poetry scene,

And would do so again!

In a brilliant venue,

The Knysna poets,

Used to meet,

At Vinyl on main!

But alas,

My life was

To change

And never to be

The same again!

To cut a long story short,

Without too much to say!

Ended up having to

Leave South Africa,

Now in Glasgow

I am based

And working in

Stavanger, Norway!

Just been through a winter

In the Northern hemisphere!

Wearing thermal underwear

And other warm gear!

But relatively speaking

Still in good cheer!

Working twelve hours a day,

An adjustment to my head

But happier now,

Than when I used to

Jump back into bed!

Now motivated

At new things, places

And people taking looks!

Busy working

On my own projects,

In my own time

And creating

Poetry books!

Got many

Friends in Glasgow

And such a great

Poetry scene!

Live music,

Second to none!

And a real vibrant scene!

My how things can change,

And circumstances

Rearrange!

Now working

Twelve hours a day!

On a ten on,

Four off rotation

When away,

I get little play!

But on the bright side,

I am flying home

To Scotland!

From Norway,

At

Three thirty

Today!

Two!

Went to get a denture repair

At Glasgow Geggies,

Cosmetic denture design,

Standing outside the shop,

Having a smoke,

Without me

Bottom dentures,

Not smiling,

Or feeling fine!

Just reading their sign!

Then this woman

Like a Black crab,

Scuttled over the pavement,

To squat right next to me!

She looked rough,

That much I could see!

She then put a large

Lighter fuel container

Up to her lip,

Then proceeded

To take either

A breath of it,

Or a sip?

She had

Two cylinders of it,

A big problem,

Without a doubt!

Having two of them,

In case the one runs out!

Where was her head?

With all these solvents,

Poisons and gases,

Running through her

Bloodstream,

Body and brain!

The act of doing it,

In public is in

Itself Insane!

What a pity, so sad!

"Can I take a photo of you?"

I asked,

Then she stuck her

Tongue out to show,

That she was bad!

The words going

Through my mind,

Like lyrics,

For a song!

"This lady is not

Going to live long!"

"Can I have a fag?"

She asked of me,

Then thinking,

If I give her one,

It could create a calamity!

Sucking on her lighter fuel

Through a canister

Instead of a cup,

I told her,

If I give you a

Lit cigarette after

You swallowing that,

You are likely

To blow up!

Felt very sorry

For her situation,

At one time

She would have been

Someone's sister,

Mother or Honey,

Bent down and

Gave her

Some money!

Was that

A wise thing to do?

Will she buy food?

Or another

Can,

Or

Two?

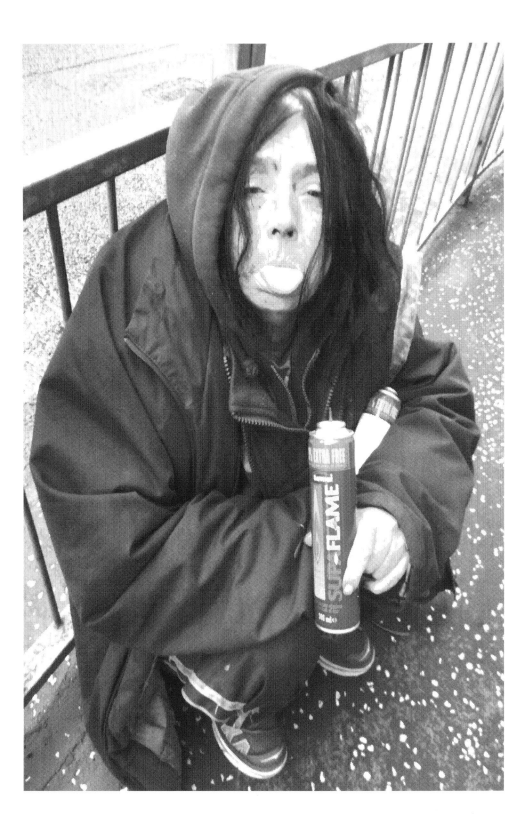

Ultimately!

We are now

Being forced

To accept an

Untested

Technology!

To allow us to have

Faster

Download speeds

On the Internet,

It is known as

5G!

Using millimetre waves

Used for crowd control

By The military!

This is being

Rolled out

Globally!

With transmitters

About every

Five hundred feet,

Beaming microwave

Energy!

These waves kill plants,

Bushes, flowers

And trees!

All insect life

And our sole

Life giving

Pollinators

The bees!

Creating

In humans

Many a

Dis-ease!

We don't have a say,

The corporations

Are having their way!

Also used for spying,

With governments lying!

That much the people

Can see!

Forever changing

The balance of nature,

And mankind's future

On this planet,

Ultimately!

Underground!

Waiting at

The station,

Silence,

All around,

Then

An

Ever

Increasing

Rumbling

Sound,

As the train

Rapidly

Pulls in,

And brakes,

On the

Glasgow

Underground!

Universe!

Met up with a Kenyan lady

Called Conso online,

I used to work there,

So, we had

Good conversations

All is fine!

Showed her a shirt

That was made for me,

By a man called Raj,

From an overland campsite,

Called Niaberi,

Outside Eldoret,

Where I built a house

In a tree!

It was a beautiful

Red tartan,

Made from an original

Massai shuka!

Red tartan wrap,

It was stolen,

So, I wondered

Could I

Make another one?

And get that

Lovely shirt back!

So, she searched

All the markets,

Till she found

The right one,

For her this

Was not easy,

It was not fun!

Negotiated

A discounted price

From the seller,

As we were now

Buying in bulk,

As I decided to make

A kilt from them as well,

As my existing one

No longer fitted,

My expanded

Stomachs bulk!

Toing and froing

With Moneygram,

Which did not work,

Now we were

In a jam,

Then a Western Union

Transfer

Bought ten of them for me!

Now for the shipping costs

By DHL

Which was

Quite expensive

You see!

As it is air mail,

Guaranteed

Two day

Delivery!

Turns out

That it

Was expensive,

Ah well,

What the hell!

Will end up with a

Unique tartan kilt,

The story,

To my

Grandchildren

I can tell!

Now

Telling this story

In rhythm, metre

And poetic verse,

All being well,

I will have the only

Nicoll/Massai kilt!

In the whole

Darn

Universe!

Vertically!

These great Apes

In Africa,

Are under threat!

Getting hunted by

Many poachers

For Bush meat

To environmentalists

And humanitarians

Regret!

Now kept in

A sanctuary!

Imitating

Their keepers,

As you

Can see!

And

Standing

Vertically!

Vinci!

"Painting is poetry

That is seen

Rather than felt,

And

Poetry is painting

That is felt

Rather than seen."

These words

By a master,

Whose works

To this day,

We can see!

They were

Said by

Leonardo

Da Vinci!

Waltzin the pencil!

(To the tune of Waltzing Matilda!
Written in the early eighties about working
As a contract draughtsman in
Process Plant, Johannesburg, South Africa.)

Once a jolly draughtsman
Booked in half an hour late,
I`ll book the full day
So, bollocks said he,
As he sang and he danced
And waltzed off to his drawing board,
I`ll invoice for ten
But only work for three!

Up jumped a Scotsman
And scribbled on his clocking card
You'll no fiddle time,
When I'm around said he
And he sang and he danced
As he clocked the man a quarter hour
"You'll go a walking the streets Jimmy!"

Back came the good times
Hourly rates increased in town
Off went the draffies,
One, two, three!
And Bills ghost can be heard
In the vaulted halls
Of Process Plant

"Why does naebody want

Tae work fir me?"

He`s Waltzin the pencil

Waltzin the pencil,

You'll go a waltzin the pencil wi me,

As he sang and he danced

And he clocked his man

The quarter hour

"You'll go a walkin

The streets Jimmy!"

What are these long white streaks in the sky?

Chorus:

What are these long white streaks in the sky?

Being spread by many planes way up high!

They are not contrails!

They spread all over the sky!

Geoengineering, solar radiation management

Playing God with nature, controlling the weather!

Being done by the UN, without asking anyone

Or even having a blether!

Spreading Nano particulates of barium and strontium,

Also, lots of Aluminium!

Why would they do this? You ask with a frown

Knowing that Agenda 21s purpose

Is to bring the world population down!

Chorus

Everyone can see them

Spreading all over the global skies!

To cut down on sunlight supposedly

Playing God in disguise!

Denying everything, doing it on the sly!

As all can see it that have an eye!

Apart from the majority

Who neither care nor see!

That our fate is linked

To these airborne particles most definitely!

Chorus

We must all come together

To fight this insanity!

Join anti geoengineering groups

On Facebook most definitely!

If not, then your future will be decided

By others who would cut your life short

And seal your destiny!

Don't let them do this

As we were all born

And God willing will

Remain alive and free!

Chorus instrumental and end.

Wit and me!

There's no many

Things better in life,

As far as I can see,

Than to swop

Each other's

Artistry,

Prose

Or

Poetry!

So here we are

Doing just that,

Jim Ferguson,

Glaswegian

Poet,

Author,

Wit

And me!

Wolf!

What we are doing
Is like crying "Wolf,"
Not for our own
Profit or bidding!
We are crying
"Wolf"
To all the
Other people
On this
Beautiful planet
That don't know,
What these
Long white streaks
In the sky are
And we
Are not
Kidding!

Photo by Stevie Brown, member of Anti geoengineering Scotland, note how there are sprays coming out where there are no engines, this proves that it is not possible for the trails to be CONtrails.

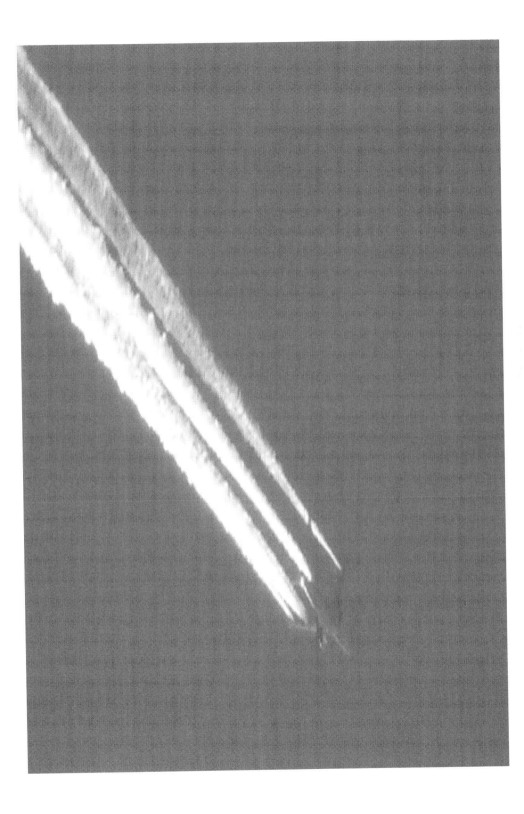

Work?

Was a friend

With Abdul,

Who was

A Turk!

He asked an

Interesting

Question!

"If you put a

Gay guy,

Into a

Straitjacket

Will it

Work?

Write up for Book launch for David Nicoll, Thoughts and Reflections Vol 3.

To save time during this launch, I thought it better to explain my background and creative process in this write up.

I moved to South Africa in February 1982 after meeting a very unhappy older man who was a workmate in the drawing office at the BP oil refinery in Grangemouth.

He told me how he had been in a place called South Africa and had to return to Scotland after five years as his wife was homesick and he was now living in a third floor flat in Falkirk and catching the bus to work each day.

He told me of how you could arrange a Braai (barbeque) in a months' time and know that it would be sunshine. He also told me about the big pieces of meat that they would cook and big gardens that were an extension of the house. Also, that some people had pools! What kind of pools? Swimming pools!

Well, that did it for me as I was sick of the Scottish winter weather and the only people that I knew that had swimming pools in their back gardens were Hollywood film stars.

So, I sent my CV to an agent in Johannesburg, got offered a job and applied for immigration. Got it and then told my new wife and my mother that we were going to South Africa.

This started the greatest adventure in my life.

Since moving there, I have worked all over South Africa and in Kenya and Tanzania as well.

Africa gets to you, it is such an amazing continent with such diverse beauty, landscapes, people and wildlife.

Of course, the sun shining almost all the time is also a bonus.

Poetry only emerged in my life at the age of twenty-eight, while trying to get rid of thoughts and emotions in my head, I sat down with pen and paper and it came out as poetry.

It was not something that I planned, it just happened that way.

Found that once you have written something down that it clears the head as well and that you can then move on.

Started initially reciting my poetry at TJs folk club in Johannesburg in the late nineties.

Then formed a band with three of the folk club performers, we were called Hakuna matata and recorded a CD called Ecology which to date has not yet been released. We played at some local festivals and were lucky enough to get to play at WOMAD when they did it in Benoni.

After moving for work to Newcastle in KwaZulu-Natal and finding that there was no live entertainment in town. I started with others, the Newcastle Folk n Culture club where people would come and play guitars, sing and recite poetry, we even had a bagpiper.

This eventually was the core for a band called US (United Souls), we played at many music festivals and recorded a CD called US Live, which has also not yet been released.

There are some tracks from both these CDs on David Nicoll and friends Vol 1.

Having met many great friends/musicians in my time in SA, whenever we would get together in studios or festivals we would record tracks for our moments in time. You can hear these on Vols. 2 and 3.

There is a very varied selection of musical styles on these CDs. I have written quite a bit about African wildlife on land and in the oceans with tracks like The Wildlife at the Zoo, Now, Man and the Whale, The Gratitude of the Humpback Whale and The Dolphins to name a few.

There are also tracks relating to Man and his effect on our beautiful planet and all its inhabitants, tracks like What we leave behind and Oh Mother Earth.

Poetry is very like music if it is written in rhythm, metre and rhyme and fits in superbly with many facets and styles of music.

Another new concept for me was as a lyricist, which also was not planned.

Gave a copy of my first book titled Thoughts and Reflections to a retired singer songwriter called Mervyn Fuller. He called me after a month and said "Listen to this, I have just made a song from one of your poems!"

Well, that was the start of a very fruitful and creative phase for both of us.

After that he would phone me from time to time, almost monthly and say," Can you write lyrics for………. And came up with many subjects. This would spark me and then I would sit down and tap inside for the poetry/lyrics and chorus.Would then type them and send them to him. He would then decide what type of song this should be? Rock, reggae, Soul, easy listening etc. and formulate the music to go with the lyrics. After he had the song recorded, he would then call in his friends Mike Laatz on Saxophone (RIP Mike) and Mike Pregnolatu on Lead guitar and they would add their magic to the song. We did this for over five years continuously and created six CDs, we were known as MAD, Mervyn And Dave and like Bernie Taupin and Elton John, never performed together, we used to live over 1000kms apart.

Please have a look at the track titles in the CDs and listen to whatever ones that resonate with you.

About creating books, this was sparked by the death of the mother of my children. It came as a shock and made me realize my own mortality and ask myself "What do I still have to do?"

Publish a book was the answer, so this started me searching through the many, many poems that I had written to select ones to publish in this book. Don't know if you have ever tried to find a publisher for a book of poetry that is not just a vanity publisher but it is not easy, so I decided just to go direct to a printer in Pietermaritzburg and took it from there, it started as a very large ring bound monstrosity with plastic covers to a normal size book after many proof reading and refining sessions.

The cover photograph for this book was taken by my friend Michael de Saedeleer, it was taken on the surface of a canal in Manchester where I was sitting on a rail bridge above and spat into the water. (RIP Mike) We had both been in England together doing contract piping draughtsman work. Incidentally this book contains a letter from President Nelson Mandela after he read the poem titled Peace and Harmony which I had sent him.

Writing POKEs POetic joKEs has been a pleasure in my life as I love to make people happy and laugh, this was the next book to be released simply called POKEs.

Met a lady in Durban one time who told me that I should have a website and that she designed them, so for several years I would put poetry together with matching photographs which I had taken, and she would load them onto the website.

After returning to Scotland last August after over thirty-six years in Africa, I got busy again sorting through more recent poetry and have released several books. They are Thoughts and Reflections Vol 2, South African tattoos which used to be on a body art/tattoos section of the website, The Poetic Picture book Vol.`s 1 & 2 which are some of the images and poetry from the website and now Thoughts and Reflections Vol 3.

My son Mark has helped me to set up a new website here which is www.davidnicoll.co.uk, there are links to all the books and CDs there, performance videos of others and myself and a new Northern Hemisphere body art /tattoos section which is growing rapidly and an ongoing project.

After returning to Scotland already having been aware of long white streaks in the sky in South Africa, saw many more in the Glasgow sky. Met up with a Mr G Bulman who had been photographing them for years here and along with Mr Ji Albagubrath we formed a group called SMAAPP Scottish Musicians and Artistes Against the Poisoning of our Planet on Facebook to try to raise awareness about the threats that they pose to humanity and indeed all lifeforms on the planet. Please join us if you too care about the future of your children and grandchildren.

With best wishes

David

Yes!

"Do you
Accept cards?"
I asked
The large
Breasted
Barmaid,
Who's hair
Was a mess!
She replied
"Me, no!
But the pub
Yes!"

Printed in Poland
by Amazon Fulfillment
Poland Sp. z o.o., Wrocław

49887869R00171